3 1705 00327 5630

Online Community Information

Creating a Nexus at Your Library

JOAN C. DURRANCE
KAREN E. PETTIGREW

D1118330

AMERICAN LIBRARY ASSOCIATION
Chicago and London
2002

STATE LIBRARY OF
SEO REGIONAL LIBRARY
CALDWELL, OHIO 43724

While extensive effort has gone into ensuring the reliability of information appearing in this book, the publisher makes no warranty, express or implied, on the accuracy or reliability of the information, and does not assume and hereby disclaims any liability to any person for any loss or damage caused by errors or omissions in this publication.

Online Community Information: Creating a Nexus at Your Library presents the highlights of a 1998–2000 IMLS National Leadership Grant, "Help-Seeking in an Electronic World: The Role of the Public Library in Helping Citizens Obtain Community Information over the Internet." The project was supported by a grant from the Institute of Museum and Library Services under the National Leadership Grants for Libraries Program, Research and Demonstration. The contents of the report do not carry the endorsement of the Institute of Museum and Library Services. The opinions expressed in the report are those of the research team.

Composition by ALA Editions in Novarese and Sabon using QuarkXPress 4.1 for the PC

Printed on 50-pound white offset, a pH-neutral stock, and bound in 10-point coated cover stock by McNaughton & Gunn

The paper used in this publication meets the minimum requirements of American National Standard for Information Sciences—Permanence of Paper for Printed Library Materials, ANSI Z39.48-1992. ∞

ISBN: 0-8389-0823-3

Copyright © 2002 by the American Library Association. All rights reserved except those which may be granted by Sections 107 and 108 of the Copyright Revision Act of 1976.

Printed in the United States of America

06 05 04 03 02   5 4 3 2 1

CONTENTS

 PREFACE

Community information (CI) helps people cope with problems of daily living and facilitates community participation by bringing people and organizations together. As a service provided by public libraries since the early 1970s, it includes three broad subcategories of information: survival or human services information, local information, and citizen action information. Thus it includes such information as healthcare, financial assistance, housing, transportation, education, and childcare services, along with information on employment opportunities, recreation programs, non-profit organizations, citizen groups, community events, and all levels of government. The specialized nature of CI services requires professional staff trained in CI collection, management, and dissemination—activities in which librarians excel. Through CI public libraries contribute to improving the quality of life for individuals in communities throughout the country.

Public libraries can facilitate citizens' access to CI by supporting community-wide information initiatives with local service providers. The Internet, along with high-speed personal computers, modems, and graphical interfaces, has suggested new ways for libraries to facilitate citizens' information needs through distributed CI systems. One such digital collaboration in which libraries have taken a leading role that is flourishing throughout the world is electronic community networking. Since the late 1980s some libraries have played pivotal roles in developing community networks that provide citizens with equitable access to the Internet for obtaining CI and communicating with others. Often organized and designed by librarians, these digital networks provide citizens with one-stop shopping by using community-oriented discussions, question-and-answer forums, access to governmental, social services, and local information, email, and Internet access. While individuals may interact with other users by posting queries, monitoring discussions, and so on, CI is a central network feature that appears in many forms. Libraries, for example, may mount their databases on the Internet, while individual service providers may post information about their programs and services. Thus the architecture of the Internet makes digital CI possible by linking information files created not only by single organizations such as libraries, but also by agencies, organizations, and individuals throughout the community (and, of course, the world). These systems enable people to access CI anytime in any place, including the home, office, or public library. The success of these initiatives, however, in facilitating citizens' access to needed services hinges both on the participation of libraries and service providers and their use and support by the intended audience, that is, the public.

Online Community Information: Creating a Nexus at Your Library presents the highlights of a 1998–2000 Institute of Museum and Library Services National Leadership Grant study, "Help-Seeking in an Electronic World: The Role of the Public Library in Helping Citizens Obtain Community Information over the Internet." This study has focused the energies of researchers from the University of Michigan and the University of Washington. Using qualitative research methods, this research examined the ways that public libraries harness the power of the Internet to provide digitized CI to their communities and explored public library involvement in community networks. It is the most extensive study ever conducted of public library provision of CI in electronic formats, public library participation in community networking, and the benefits these activities bring to American communities.

Beyond examining general trends in CI service provision in libraries across the country, we focused in-depth on how public libraries are harnessing the power of the Internet to provide CI in digitized forms through community networking initiatives. In this effort, we focused on the perceptions and expectations of:

Individuals who access CI on the Internet

Librarians who assist individuals with Internet searches for CI

Library administrators and staff who are involved in community networking on behalf of the library

Service providers who post information about their services on community networks

Thus, goals 1–4 of our project were as follows:

Goal 1: To gather systematic evidence of citizens' online information behavior while searching for CI on the Internet (these impact indicators included users' perceptions and expectations)

Goal 2: To compare citizens' perceptions and expectations of electronic CI with those of service providers who post that information on the Internet

Goal 3: To investigate the role of librarians in assisting the public with Internet searches for CI

Goal 4: To determine the organizational impact of public library participation in community networking for the purpose of informing future evaluation

Best practices were also identified for emulation in other libraries and communities. Hence, goal 5 was as follows:

Goal 5: To identify best practices at electronic CI provision for emulation by other public libraries and communities

Our study was guided by nine research questions that focused on the perceptions and expectations of different stakeholders regarding networked CI and community networking. These nine questions were grouped in terms of three headings: users, service providers, and the public library. Over the course of our study, some research questions were broadened while others were consolidated to facilitate the attainment of our proposed goals.

Users:

1. What situations prompt individuals to use the Internet for obtaining CI, and what specific types of help are they seeking?
2. What barriers do users encounter and how do they get around them?
3. What do users do with CI they obtain electronically through the library (i.e., how does the CI help?)?

Service Providers:

4. How do service providers perceive posting information on the Internet will help clients and their organizations, and how do their perceptions relate to those of the public?

The Public Library:

5. How are public libraries participating in community networking, and how do librarians expect participation will help clients and benefit communities?
6. How has library Internet access to CI affected traditional reference service?
7. What specific tools and processes do librarians require for evaluating the organizational impact of (a) library Internet access to CI; and (b) library participation in community networking?
8. What best practices for library participation in community networking and Internet access to CI can be identified that will benefit other libraries and communities?
9. What tools can be developed that will facilitate these best practices?

Our detailed, unprecedented approach comprised two phases. In phase 1 we conducted a two-stage national survey. The first survey was sent to a stratified sample of medium and large-sized libraries throughout the country. That survey, sent to the directors of 725 libraries, had a 70% response rate with 505 responses and provided baseline data about the penetration of CI services at the end of the century. The second survey was sent to those identified by the library directors as coordinators of their libraries' CI activities (N = 227). It consisted of a sixteen-page, seventy-four-question instrument that focused in detail on all aspects of provision of CI in 1999. A key finding from the survey was that a majority of libraries are providing CI in distributed, digitized forms for which community networks are a primary vehicle.

For phase 2 we conducted intensive case studies of public library–community networking systems in three communities—Northeastern Illinois, Pittsburgh, and Portland, Oregon—that are nationally recognized for their respective community network in which the local public library system plays a leading role. At each site we used triangulated methods to study the perceptions and expectations of community network users, service providers who post information about their agencies on community networks, CI librarians, and library administrators involved with community networking. Our data-collection methods included online surveys and follow-up interviews with 197 network users along with in-depth interviews and focus groups with 87 staff members from public libraries and social service agencies.

Using these multiple methods, we gathered systematic evidence of citizens' online information behavior while searching for CI on the Internet; examined and compared citizens' and service providers' perceptions and expectations of networked CI; investigated the role of librarians in providing digital CI as well as assistance in its use; examined and determined a range of impacts of library participation both in the provision of digital CI and as partners in community networking for the purpose of informing future evaluation; and identified best practices at electronic CI provision for emulation by other public libraries and communities. Moreover, we identified ways of operationalizing "information communities," an emergent concept used to describe virtual and physical communities that are based on solid aspects of information gathering and provision. A key finding from our work is that CI librarians are challenged with finding ways to evaluate their services effectively. Our results lay the groundwork for developing such tools in the future.

In the following chapters we document how public library participation in networked CI services is benefiting individuals, local service providers, and libraries—as institutions—by enhancing the quality of life in American communities in both urban and rural areas. In appendix A and B, respectively, we review a large body of interdisciplinary work that is related to our study, and discuss our research design and specific methods. Additional details of the study, including surveys, results, and interview guides, are available on the project website, http://www.si. umich.edu/libhelp/, as well as other reports listed in our bibliography.

Joan C. Durrance
Karen E. Pettigrew

ACKNOWLEDGMENTS

As principal investigators of this research, we would like to extend our public thanks to those people who made this research a success. We owe a debt of gratitude to the Help Seeking in an Electronic World research assistants (RAs), Michael Jourdan, and Karen Scheuerer (University of Michigan). These talented graduate students made strong contributions to the project from the design of the instruments, through the data collection and analysis, and in the presentation of data. Karen and Michael were invaluable in helping us collect stories and develop profiles and case studies. They created the project website and made sure that its wealth of best-practice data has been accessible.

We would also like to thank the graduate student RAs who have become part of Help Seeking's successor research project, IMLS-funded How Libraries and Librarians Help—doctoral student Kent Unruh (University of Washington) and master's students Christopher Hamilton and Erica Olsen (University of Michigan) who assisted in the completion of this final report. These RAs along with project manager Karen Scheuerer designed and developed the project's updated website, http://www.si.umich.edu/libhelp/ and effectively incorporated relevant content from the Help Seeking project.

We also wish to thank the community network staff and library administrators who hosted us on our site visits to Three Rivers Free-Net (Carnegie Library of Pittsburgh), NorthStarNet (North Suburban and Suburban Library Systems), and CascadeLink (Multnomah County Public Library) and who, along with the many individuals we interviewed, provided us with invaluable data on the benefits of community networks. We wish to extend our thanks to the Social Science and Humanities Research Council of Canada (SSHRC) for awarding Karen Pettigrew a postdoctoral fellowship at the University of Michigan, as well as the staff of many non-profit organizations, local government agencies, citizens, and local public libraries who responded to our website surveys and participated in interviews and observations. Finally, we wish to thank IMLS for the opportunity to conduct this major study.

1

How the Public Uses Networked Community Information

In this chapter we draw upon findings from our online surveys with community network users and follow-up interviews in the case studies to address the following research questions: (1) what situations prompt citizens to use the Internet for obtaining community information (CI), and what types of help are they seeking? (2) what barriers do users encounter and how do they get around them? And (3) what do users do with CI that they obtain electronically (i.e., how does the CI help?)? These questions coincide with our study's objective of investigating citizens' information behavior when using public library–community networks for daily problem-solving.

As will be discussed in chapter 2, we conducted an online survey with 197 users of our three case-study community networks, followed by in-depth telephone interviews with a subset of 27 survey respondents. Both instruments were based on Dervin's sense-making theory (cf 1992), which focuses on the uses that individuals make of information systems and the barriers that they encounter. Our broad finding that users equally represented both genders, are employed in a range of occupations, and whose ages follow a normal distribution confirms that all citizens need information about social services, transportation, education, and so on, at some point in their daily lives.

Why People Use the Internet
for Community Information

I really like the huge number of local sites organized in a coherent manner. You just can't find things like local movie listings quickly on the big search engines. To find a church in my neighborhood or to locate my local congressman or to see where they offer swing dance class in my neck of the woods, the community network is the place to go (female community network user, age 26–35).

Our respondents reported that they use networked CI systems for many different types of situations, including those of a personal nature and those regarding the workplace. This confirms a tenet of information behavior, namely that all individuals require CI at one point or another and that it is the individual's situation that reveals most insight into information seeking and use (Harris & Dewdney 1994). We found that users seek the following types of digital CI (in alphabetical order):

Business

Computer and technical
information

Education

Employment opportunities

Financial support

Governmental and civic

Health

Housing

Library operations and services

Local events

Local history and genealogy

Local information (local ac-
commodations, community
features)

Local news (weather, traffic,
school closures)

Organizations and groups

Other people (both local and
beyond the community)

Parenting

Recreation and hobbies

Sale, exchange, or donation of
goods

Social services

Volunteerism

These categories are markedly different from those traditionally used to classify CI needs. Moreover, they also broaden findings reported by Bishop et al. (1999). Notable differences between our categories and those reported in CI studies conducted prior to the Internet are: (1) a strong emphasis on employment opportunities, volunteerism, and social service availability; and (2) the inclusion of new categories such as items for sale, local history and genealogy, local news, computer and technical information, and other people (residing both within and beyond the community).

What is the reason for this emphasis on employment information and so on, and the emergence of novel categories? Our analysis indicates that the Internet is responsible. Increased computer capabilities and online connectivity have enabled many different types of service providers to make information available about themselves that was previously unavailable or only in limited amounts via a public library's CI record. In other words, service providers are now able to share information about themselves first-hand. Prior to the Internet, such information was largely only available on paper and had to be searched manually and often through intermediaries (although many public libraries maintained electronic, in-house databases, these databases were seldom available to the public for direct end-user searching). The breadth of CI available, along with new search engine and software capabilities, has contributed to extending the notion of what CI comprises. Just as the Internet is broadening our concept of community, so it is changing the scope of CI. Due to networked CI systems, people can search for other people online, sell and trade goods, research their family history, exchange neighborhood information—and all at a faster, more immediate pace. Increased access to the Internet, and hence community network, especially via public libraries has led to an increased public awareness of what's available, what's going on, and what might be found in a community. This enhanced access is undoubtedly facilitating CI flow. Whereas people once relied on conversations over backyard fences, postings on notice boards at supermarkets, and local newspapers, they are now drawing upon the capabilities of the Internet, as fueled by public library efforts, to seek and share information about their communities.

While the above categories are useful for understanding the types of networked CI that users seek, further insights are gained when one considers the actual situations. The following are just a few examples:

> Teenagers used the network to find summer employment because it has all the local job information in one place and is trusted as a reliable, current source.

> A senior citizen used the network to find out about an important upcoming town council meeting.

> A man looking for a local directory of gay and lesbian organizations searched the Web but only came across national resources. The network directed him to the exact local organization he needed.

A homebound person used the network to research his family's genealogy because of its comprehensive organization of local resources,
including public library, county agency, and local historical association materials.

A former resident organized a family reunion from across the country
using the network to arrange everything from activities to hotels.

A woman used the network to learn about local government information, such as current ordinances pertaining to matters ranging
from trash pickup to flood damage prevention, and to identify
sources of funding for a community-service project intended to
help a nearby low-income community.

A man, who sometimes uses the network to find miscellaneous information, said he uses it "mostly for help with lung cancer and possible cures or ways of living longer whether it be conventional or
alternative medicine."

According to the sense-making theory, information needs cannot be
considered in isolation from the situations that create them since any situation is likely to yield multiple information needs, that is, information
found for one aspect of a query frequently opens another related information need. As we found, the situations for which users sought digital CI
were complex and usually required multiple pieces of information. In this
sense, our users described how their searches were on-going and how they
anticipated having to pose several different queries or consult multiple
sources. This notion of the on-going search is similar to Bates' "berrypicking" concept where users search for information "a bit at a time" and
alter their search strategies according to what they find and what barriers
they encounter (1989). There are several implications of this behavior for
CI system design, which we discuss at the end of this chapter.

Enabling Aspects of Community Information

Beyond analyzing the CI that users sought by need category and situation
type, we also focused on the information's enabling aspects, that is, the
attributes of the information that would aid users in whatever it was they
were trying to accomplish. This approach builds on Dervin's notion of
"verbings." We derived the following "information enabling" categories
for classifying the types of CI requested:

Comparing (similar to verifying but may come earlier in the cognitive process)

Connecting (how to find people with related interests, etc.)

Describing (services offered, cost, eligibility, etc.)

Directing (information about where something is located or how to get somewhere)

Explaining (in-depth, content-oriented information that explains how something works)

Problem solving (information that will help bridge a gap or solve a problem)

Promoting (want others to know about them, e.g., that they're available for employment, that they've started a new club, etc.)

Relating (information that is relevant to the individual's needs and construct)

Trusting (information that the individual feels comes from a trusted source. This is similar to high-quality—something that people said they wanted)

Verifying (a form of corporate intelligence, people want to keep up with what their competition is doing, be aware of new trends, etc.)

These "enabling" attributes provide a novel way of viewing information needs because they focus on what users are trying to accomplish for a particular situation. When considered in conjunction with (1) the user's initial need (as presented to the digital CI system by either pointing and clicking or by typing a search phrase); (2) the situation that prompted that need; and (3) what is known about the barriers that users encounter—as discussed later—these enabling categories reveal several implications for the design of digital CI systems.

Other Findings regarding the Public's Online Information Behavior

Several other novel themes emerged regarding citizens' online information behavior that contribute to the literature and may aid in networked CI system design. For example, respondents indicated that they often tried other sources (e.g., friends, newspapers, telephone directories, etc.) for help with their questions before turning to the system. Such was the case of a user from Pittsburgh, who accessed the Three Rivers Free-Net (TRFN) after friends and co-workers told him that it contained job listings, and other sources such as local newspapers proved unsuccessful. Since the 1960s, information science research has indicated that social ties and face-to-face communication are primary sources of information, regardless of the setting (home, workplace, school, etc.). Our findings suggest that this remains the case: the Internet has not replaced the role of social ties in citizens' information behavior. During our interviews, several respondents described how they spoke about their information need or situation with a social tie before searching online. Thus we found that the Internet is supplementing other information-seeking behaviors in addition to creating new pathways for obtaining information: people are using networked CI systems as an additional source. Moreover, we learned that people want their community networks to promote social interaction by bringing people together. This notion was expressed well by a user who said: "A bulletin board or some way to facilitate people meeting each other and getting around would be very helpful. I've recently moved to town and am looking for ways to meet people. Maybe a place where people could find others who are interested in a supper club or playing cards, or informal sporting groups, etc."

Users also tended to be highly confident that they could find what they needed through the community network. Despite the difficulties with using the Internet noted in previous studies, such as lack of content, low retrieval rates with search engines, inaccurate information, and so on, our respondents tended to perceive their community network as a ubiquitous source and gateway to all knowledge. In this sense we identified a mismatch between what users think they can obtain via the Internet and the likelihood that that information exists and can be easily located. This finding expands on a principle of everyday information behavior: that a mismatch exists between what users believe service providers offer and what they actually do (Harris & Dewdney 1994). Another plausible explanation is that users are transferring their mental model of what public libraries contain and how they function to the Internet in general. In other words, of community networks and the Internet, users hold the same "information" expectations that they associate with public libraries. The difficulty here, of course, is that public libraries and the Internet are not the same thing: they provide different sorts of information in vastly different ways, with the roles played by professional librarians making a critical difference. This finding was recently supported by Roger and D'Elia (2000). An interesting and representative example of users' perceptions of the Internet and community networks was expressed by a young man who asserted that the Internet and community network provided non-biased information. Later, acknowledging that sometimes information is "sensationalized," he added that he tries to balance information retrieved from the Internet with that gleaned from other sources before making a final decision.

On a different theme, it was interesting how some respondents revealed that they were searching for CI on behalf of another person (e.g., relative, friend), and not always at that person's behest. A man, for example, was looking for medical information for his wife, while a mother was searching for employment opportunities for her two children, and a staff member at a social-service agency said he would forward information he had come across to his co-workers. This notion of proxy searching, of gathering requested and unrequested CI for others, supports recent findings regarding the Web by Erdelez and Rioux (2000), which they describe as information encountering, and by Gross (in press), who describes how users present "imposed queries" at reference desks in public and school libraries and suggests fruitful paths for future study. On many levels, it seems that the Internet has made it easier for researchers to label and identify a particular social type, one that might be best described as "information gatherers," or "monitors," to borrow from Baker & Pettigrew (1999). In our study, these active CI seekers, who may be considered somewhat akin to information gatekeepers, appeared to relish time spent browsing and poking about the community network and the Internet. But the greatest satisfaction they described was when they found something that they believed might be of interest to someone else, which they would quickly pass on, either by email or in person. Hence, a distinguishing feature of these CI gatherers is that they may be socially connected or active and, perhaps more importantly, are aware of the potential CI needs or interests of the people with whom they interact. These CI gatherers do not wait for someone to say "I need to know about X." Instead, they take mental notes of what's going on in the lives of the people around them, their interests and situations, and then keep an eye out for CI that might be of interest or helpful—not by initiating an actual, purposive search. In this sense, CI monitors are able to recognize the potential CI needs of the people around them. Another defining element of this social type is that they do not really care if the CI they pass on is actually used, and they exhibit an understanding that sometimes information is used and proven helpful at a later point in time. For systems design, this information-gatherer social type has important implications. For example, in communities that are considered information poor, individuals who represent this social type could be identified and given advance training in Internet searching as well as in how to identify information needs and how to provide information in ways that best facilitate those needs.

We also found support for Wellman's (Hampton & Wellman 2000) notion that the Internet has created "glocalization" where it is being used by individuals for both local and long-distance interaction. In our study, respondents used the community network as a personal gateway to websites located throughout the world, while people far beyond the network's physical home were using it to obtain local information. A woman in Florida, for example, used TRFN to locate information about seniors' housing for her elderly father who was moving to the Pittsburgh area. A different user who was accessing the network from another region remarked on how it helps her connect with her family: "Although I haven't lived there in years, I can keep up with the events and what is going on." Respondents also expressed interest in having a strong regional and neighborhood emphasis in their networks' content.

In sum, our analysis of the situations that create users' needs for CI revealed a plethora of rich findings that expand on previous reports and, more importantly, signify several novel ways in which people are seeking CI at the turn of the century by drawing upon new technologies supported by public libraries.

Barriers to Using Networked CI Systems

The notion of barriers, which is central to the sense-making framework, represents the ways in which people are prevented or blocked from seeking information successfully. By identifying barriers, one can devise ways of improving the design of networked CI systems that facilitate users' information behavior. Our respondents were asked several open-ended questions that address types of barriers. Specifically, we asked them to explain what, if anything, would make it easier for them to find what they're looking for and to describe any past actions they might have taken regarding their search topic.

Our analysis revealed that users encounter several types of barriers when using community networks and the Internet in general. We labeled the main barrier as "information-related." Barriers that fell under this broad category included:

Information overload: Due to poor search engines and site indexing, users frequently complained that they retrieved too much CI and that they were challenged with discerning what was relevant to their search. Users were often daunted by a site's layout (e.g., it appeared too busy, too many bells and whistles, poor font and color choice, especially for those who are color-blind) and the amount of text displayed on a single screen. Regarding the Internet, in general, one user said he didn't "like it a lot" because most sites and search engines give him 10 billion leads that get him side-tracked until he's forgotten what it was he was looking for.

Poorly organized (classified): Users complained that they often did not find CI where they expected to find it, and that there was little cross referencing. According to one woman, "I have a difficult time finding this information. None of the [system] categories apply to this even though I know the entity exists. Search engines didn't help either."

Out-of-date and inaccurate information: Users found CI that was either out-of-date or there was no way of discerning when a page was created or last updated. Inaccuracies in content were also noted.

Authority: Without proper identifiers and author credentials or association endorsements, users said it was difficult to gauge the "quality" of the CI source, that is, whether they should trust the CI (and its source) or not.

Missing: Users sometimes complained that pages did not contain information that they described as included at the top of the document or on another page.

Dead links: Users were frustrated when finding a link to a page or site that they believe will be highly relevant to their information need, only to find that the link is inactive or otherwise unavailable.

Language used: Beyond most information appearing in English only, users also commented on how some sites contained information that was written using jargon or at a level that was too high for many to understand.

Security: Users want strong evidence that the information they submit and retrieve is confidential—"reassured security"—as one user phrased it.

Specificity: Users want to be able to search for information at the neighborhood level. As one user explained, "What's the use of providing information concerning neighborhoods if you then don't make it easy for someone to determine exactly which neighborhood they're in/belong to?"

Non-anticipatory systems: Although users were unable to articulate this barrier themselves, their responses in the surveys and interviews indicated that users' information behavior would be greatly facilitated if digital CI systems were "smart enough" either to anticipate their next information need (based on the need posed to the system by typed query or by point and click) or a related information need. All too often users described how the site they found was not quite what they were looking for but they did not know where to go to next.

These information-related barriers point to problems as well as potential solutions for improving the usability and helpfulness of networked CI systems. However, *other barriers* that users encounter also emerged from our analysis. Such barriers included:

Technological barriers: Computer connection speeds were very slow, software worked slowly or was unavailable or incompatible with connecting systems, etc. A user of the Three Rivers Free-Net, for example, described how he is unable to use the service at times because the links are slow.

Economic barriers: Users who could not afford their own computing equipment or online access felt they were at a disadvantage unless they were able to access equipment at a public library or other public computing site, which even at the best of times was still not as convenient as having a home system.

Geographic barriers: People were hindered in accessing computers because they lived far away from a public library or other public access site or because high-speed connectivity was unavailable in their area.

Search skill barriers: Community network users did not know how to search the system (or Internet in general) or how to use advanced methods. This was reflected by several respondents, one of whom commented, "I have a hard time finding information even though I think I'm a pretty savvy Web surfer."

Cognitive barriers: Users did not understand how the Internet works in terms of how it is indexed and how search engines work, how links are created, who creates and manages the information, how sites are updated, etc. As one user explained, "I am not Internet savvy enough to know what would make it easier, I just muddle through," while another remarked: "there is probably more to the website than I know about."

Psychological barriers: Users frequently expressed a lack of confidence in their own ability to find needed information. In other words, they internalized their search failures: instead of attributing them to the Internet or just a plain lack of availability, they believed the reason they could not find something was because they were unable to carry out the search successfully.

These barriers are highly significant because they represent the impediments that users encounter when seeking information. People who are job seeking, for example, feel that they cannot get ahead unless they have access to a computer, not only so they can become more computer literate but also because that's how they perceive people learn about job opportunities these days. For any one situation or information need, a user might be confronted by several barriers, which, collectively, can overwhelm the user and prevent him or her from locating needed information.

Despite the barriers that users encounter when seeking CI online, the participants in our study overwhelmingly emphasized how they have benefited from the availability of online CI via their public library–community networks. Several important themes emerged under this third research question. Most notably, users reported an increased ability to access CI. Specifically, they described how they now have:

Increased access to hard-to-get information

Increased access to "higher quality" information (i.e., more current, more comprehensive, better organized, and linked to other relevant sites)

Found information that is easier to use

Decreased transaction "costs" (saving them time, money, and energy); increased convenience; increased ability to identify trusted information

"I love the Free-Net and I'm incredibly satisfied with and grateful for the service." This user's comment reflected those made by many others who explained at length how they are benefiting from an increased ability to access information. As one user explained: "this information is not available in one spot anywhere else," while another said "good source of information with a broad basis. I recommend this site frequently, especially to those considering relocating to the area." A user accessing the system from home commented on how it provides "one easy location to hook up to the local and state government agencies." A different user remarked: "I absolutely rely on this website for home and work projects. I also refer lots of people I speak with (I'm a recruiter for the city) from out of state and locally to the website. It cuts through all the garbage and gets straight to the heart!" A woman accessing the system from work said "I use this page as my home page because it offers concise and effective access to all areas of the 'net, all organized in an understandable way. Best of all, since it is non-commercial, I feel that I'm being directed to the best sites, not just the sites that have paid for a listing."

Users also described how access to networked CI yielded *benefits at the personal, family, and neighborhood levels*. Specifically, they described how they have:

Greater confidentiality protection; greater
   comfort in asking sensitive questions

Skill and confidence building

Employment and educational gains

Increased knowledge of community

Value for family, friends, and neighborhood

Support for these themes emerged repeatedly. People explained how their local community network provided them with one-stop shopping for information about all aspects of their area and met the information needs of their entire families. One user commented on how relocating to the city was easier because of the network. He said, "I'm very glad the network is available here. It's made moving to the city much easier to deal with. I can still get in touch with friends via email, look for information and products, and generally not suffer the pangs of complete withdrawal from the T1 access I had before moving here."

Finally, users also reported benefiting from the ways in which public library–community network initiatives build community and facilitate cohesiveness both within and among different subpopulations. Specifically, they explained how:

Bridges have been built among previously unconnected
    people and groups

Increased information sharing now exists

The limits of geography have been reduced

Communication among organizations has increased

Trust among organizations has increased

Linkages, connections, and partnership opportunities
    have increased

While these advantages are linked with those reported by service providers and public library staff, and are discussed in chapter 6, the following comments by two different users sum up those made by many others: "Please let anyone involved with the network know how much the community depends on and appreciates this service," and "I believe this is the best use of funds provided."

Discussion

Our analysis of users' online information behavior reveals a rich portrait of how individuals are getting faster access to more detailed information in ways that were never possible even a decade ago, due to networked CI system initiatives. These systems are valued and used by all segments of the adult population, and enable individuals from near and far to find information about local services and events, and facilitate different types of information seeking. Our analysis of the situations that create users' needs for CI revealed a plethora of rich findings that expand on previous reports and, more importantly, signify several novel ways in which people are seeking CI at the turn of the century by drawing upon new technologies supported by public libraries. However, our results also indicated that users' mental models of what information exists, is retrievable, and is accurate on the Internet are overly optimistic. Although many barriers are associated with digital CI system access, these same barriers can reveal optimal solutions that will assist in creating even stronger and more information-literate communities. Our findings suggest the following fourteen ways in which digital CI systems might be improved:

1. Provide users with greater specificity in their searches by improving the capability of search engines and searchable fields. Users, for example, want to be able to search for CI by neighborhood and zip code, which reflects their notions of community.

2. Incorporate anticipatory search features that offer users suggestions or "next steps" on other types of information that are related to the information currently retrieved. For example, if a user is searching for genealogical information, then the system could suggest other sources of genealogical information as well as genealogical software for family-tree building, and so on.

3. Query the user automatically regarding the enabling aspects of the information that they are seeking and then use this data to provide information holistically. For example, if a user is seeking "directing" information, then the system might also bring up local bus schedules and routes, directions, and so on, through a geographic information system. If a user is seeking "connecting" information, then the system might include bulletin boards and other mechanisms that will facilitate communication and the identification of individuals.

4. Use a CI taxonomy, such as Sales (1994), for organizing and indexing CI records and make the taxonomy available online as part of the digital CI system. Records also should be indexed at the regional and neighborhood levels as that reflects how users prefer to search for CI.

5. Follow established interface design principles, such as those proposed by Head (1999) and Raskin (2000), to reduce incidents of information overload. Incorporating easy-to-use search engines that have different levels of search sophistication and following solid design standards can contribute greatly to reducing users' frustrations with pages that appear "too busy" and list too much text.

6. Indicate when the CI displayed on a page was last updated.

7. Indicate the CI source and that person's credentials.

8. Ensure that pages that contain the information indicated are displayed on a higher-level screen.

9. Remove dead links regularly.

10. Use appropriate language when providing CI that is understandable to users.

11. Provide help mechanisms that explain the very basics, that is, how

the digital CI system and Internet are organized and function, how search engines work, and explain that sometimes information is unavailable at no fault of the user.

12. Provide users with contact information (email and phone number) for someone who can assist with matching their information needs to the system and with general system use.

13. Incorporate mid-way features that allow the systems to be used by people with slower machines, and so on.

14. Incorporate more ways of linking people together to facilitate social interaction via bulletin boards, and so on.

By carefully considering the information needs and seeking behavior of users when designing digital information systems, many of the barriers noted earlier can be avoided or greatly reduced. Systems that anticipate related information needs and the actual activities or functions that users are trying to accomplish can go even further in facilitating users' online information behavior.

2

From Vertical Files to the Web
The Impact of Digital CI on Public Library Information Services

This chapter answers the research question: How has library Internet access to CI affected traditional reference service? In order to learn about provision of CI we developed an extensive survey that focused only on CI provision that was sent to those identified by the library directors as coordinators of the library's CI activities. That sixteen-page, seventy-four-question survey focused in detail on the provision of CI, including formats used, collection and management approaches, major areas of change, public access and public services, staffing, marketing and promotion, and collaboration and partnering. This chapter, based largely on the detailed responses of coordinators of library CI, shows how libraries currently provide CI. We begin with a brief overview that provides the perspective for the discussion in this chapter.

A Brief History of CI in Public Libraries

Since the 1970s, librarians have developed CI files and services in public libraries initially in public library "outreach" departments. In the early 1970s public librarians, whose expertise had previously focused on organizing the world's knowledge, applied those skills to the community's disorganized, disparate information that was squirreled away in many locations. In doing so, they came into contact more fully with governmental units, non-profit organizations, and service providers than ever before. These activities resulted in the first library CI focus, information and referral (I&R) services that were developed in response to findings that citizens were uninformed about public and private resources, facilities, rights, and programs and were frustrated with trying to obtain information for everyday problems (Childers 1984; Durrance 1984a; Kochen & Donohue 1976).

CI helps people cope with problems of daily living and facilitates community participation. Thus CI covers information about human services, that is, healthcare, financial assistance, housing, transportation, education, and childcare services; it includes information on employment opportunities, recreation programs, non-profit organizations, citizen groups, community events, and all levels of government. The staff of CI services put that information to work helping people with their quests to find new jobs, daycare services for children, meal delivery or visiting nursing for aging parents, and so forth.

During its early years CI librarians gained the skills necessary to identify, organize, and manage large, paper-based files of data about their communities. They honed question-negotiation skills to more effectively respond to everyday information needs. Along the way, they learned how to build effective databases, experimented with new information technologies, employed marketing techniques to get the word out about library I&R, and collaborated with other community organizations (Durrance & Schneider 1996). Specialized CI emerged through the provision of such library services as job centers, giving librarians additional opportunities to gain skill in collaborating with other community agencies and honing their community-building skills (Durrance 1993; 1994).

During this same period, external funding enabled researchers to study ways that CI services might facilitate the practice of public librarianship (including reference) as well as service evaluation, and heralded the systematic study of citizens' everyday information behavior. In 1984, Tom Childers reported that 68% of public libraries nationwide offered CI services as part of their standard service, and that another 28% offered them at the discretion of a library staff member. The years since Childers' landmark study witnessed many advancements in how public libraries deliver CI. Beyond the *PLA Guidelines for Establishing Community Information and Referral Services in Public Libraries* (1997 marked its fourth edition), databases and software were designed specifically for handling CI, and taxonomies (e.g., Sales' *Taxonomy of Human Services*) were developed for indexing CI records.

In the 1980s the Internet made electronic community networks possible. The World Wide Web revolution in the mid-1990s provided unprecedented opportunities for librarians to organize CI and add value to networked CI. Due to the distributed nature of the Web and this new opportunity to demonstrate their unique skills of information organization, librarians were suddenly seen as CI providers. Therefore, most of this chapter focuses on this important recent transformation, the public library's Internet presence.

The Public Library Web Presence

Our study shows that in 1999, 81% of 498 public libraries had a website. We found that, in general, libraries were far more likely to place information about the library on the website than they were to provide information about the community. Tables 2.1 and 2.2 show this pattern.

Although we found that public library websites were more likely to concentrate on library-focused information, we did find that across all libraries, nearly three quarters provide links to information on the community developed by other organizations. Fewer were likely to provide

TABLES 2.1 and 2.2

Community Information Content on Public Library Websites	
Links to information on the community developed by others	71%
Links to library-developed web pages	41%
Information about community events	28%
Library CI databases	26%
Link to local community network	22%
Digitized local special collection	16%
Links to digitized special collection	15%
"Library Focused" Content on Public Library Websites	
General information about the library	97%
Information about library programs and services	92%
OPAC	75%
Electronic resources available to patrons	71%

links to library-developed community web pages, information about community events, library-developed CI databases, links to local community networks, digitized special collections created by the library, or links to digitized special collections created by other organizations.

Public Library Websites: The Public Library's Premiere Marketing Tool

Web pages have become the public library's major public face to the community and the world. Most CI librarians make use of this as a primary marketing tool. The library's website is used more heavily than their other marketing mechanisms—articles in the local newspaper, news releases, and articles in the library's newsletter.

The Web brings public libraries an exponential expansion of their audience. The *New York Review of Books* reported in 1999 that the New York Public Library "dispenses so much information electronically to readers all over the world that it reports ten million hits on its computer system each month as opposed to 50,000 books dispensed in its reading room at 42nd Street" (Roberts 1999). In the fall of 2000 the Three Rivers Free-Net (TRFN), the community network developed by the Carnegie Library of Pittsburgh, reported more than 87,000 average hits and 9,000 average visitor sessions to TRFN per day (TRFN website, Dec. 7, 2000).

Well-designed public library web pages send strong, clear messages about the library's various roles (including providing CI) as well as its resources, services, and intended audiences. Effective public library websites tend to reflect both the virtual and the physical library. They put information most valuable to the user at the top level, show the potential user how this website can be valuable to him or her, provide navigational cues, and use terms that people understand.

Commonly used website features include information about the library and the site, detailed information about the library's collections, descriptions of library services and programming, information about special, user-centered services (including teens, seniors, book clubs, etc.), interactive features including feedback mechanisms and digital reference, and information about the community.

While we identified some fine examples of best practice sites, we also discovered at this stage in the evolution of public library websites that a number of libraries have not fully understood the marketing power of the library's website and thus send minimal messages. Or worse, some features such as top-level links to library fines and fees reinforce negative stereotypes of libraries and librarians. Some fail to focus on the information that sets that library apart from all other libraries, information about their particular local community. Many fail to show the community that librarians are experts in question answering. If people do not know that librarians are experts in facilitating digital reference, they will not conclude that they can get valuable information about their community from public librarians.

Library Websites Facilitate Digital Reference

Library websites have the potential to send strong messages about what public libraries and librarians do for their communities. Digital reference is emerging as a powerful tool. Baltimore County Public Library reference staff described their pioneering efforts at digital reference in 1998 (Roger). We found in mid-1999 that 58% of public librarians engaged in providing CI said that people could ask reference questions on the library's website. A closer look reveals that "Ask a Librarian" features are often quite difficult to find on public library websites. The "Help Seek" project website: http://www.si.umich.edu/helpseek/ describes a number of examples of public library digital or online reference services in small, medium, and large libraries. Some of these include: Glencoe (IL) Public Library, Jackson County Library in Medford (OR), King County (WA) Public Library, Skokie (IL) Public Library, Tacoma (WA) Public Library, and San Francisco (CA) Public Library. Those that prominently display the "Ask a Question" feature, such as those of the public libraries of Toledo Lucas County (OH), St. Charles (IL), King County (WA), Santa Monica (CA), and Houston (TX), educate the public about the role of librarians, alerting people—many for the first time—that librarians are information professionals or "knowledge navigators."

Several examples that illustrate approaches to digital reference follow.

Houston Public Library Online Interactive Reference Services

http://www.hpl.lib.tx.us/hpl/interactive/eref_form.html/

An interactive feature of the Houston Public Library website, as seen in figure 2.1 below, encourages users to ask for online reference help. The site explains:

The Houston Public Library (HPL) now offers reference service through easy to use email submission forms. With the Email Reference Form, brief questions are answered, or suggestions on sources and locations are offered to help find answers to more lengthy questions. Responses are provided within 36–48 hours or less, excluding weekends. Additionally, the Email Shelf Check Form allows you to ask HPL staff to check the shelves for a particular book, CD, tape, or other type of item. If the item is in the library at the time of the request, an online request can be made to send it to the HPL location of your choice. A librarian will also notify you of the status of the requested item by email.

FIGURE 2.1　SAMPLE SCREEN FROM HOUSTON PUBLIC LIBRARY
http://www.hpl.lib.tx.us/hpl/interactive/answers.html/

Glencoe Public Library (IL) Offers Electronic Reference Resources

http://www.glencoe.lib.il.us/GckLbRef.html/

This Glencoe Public Library (GPL) offers access to a select group of websites that answer many basic reference questions by providing links to online libraries, encyclopedias, and virtual reference desks. They also include a user-friendly tutorial for searching the Web. Moreover, GPL provides library users with the chance to interact with Glencoe Library's reference staff via email to ask questions and place items on hold. Reference staff members check their email regularly and are committed to answering reference questions quickly.

Seattle Public Library Ask a Question

http://www.spl.org/quickinfo/formexpl.html/

The Seattle Public Library's Quick Information Center pledges to try to answer patrons' reference questions within twenty-four hours. They will answer a range of questions that includes biographical and historical facts, definitions, spelling and grammar, local and national events, etiquette, geography, government, holidays, movies, quotations, sports, scientific and math formulas, and more. In addition, librarians can help inquirers find people, businesses, organizations, and government offices. They are also happy to assist with questions requiring longer or more complex research by connecting citizens with the most appropriate reference department. For those Web visitors who need an immediate answer, the web page provides online frequently needed quick facts, usually pertaining to local and government information, community organizations, and events.

Danbury Public Library

http://www.danburylibrary.org/new/forms/ask.html/

The Danbury Public Library encourages library patrons to send reference questions from home or work. Any library card-holder or Danbury resident can submit questions via a user-friendly web form or via email. The librarians respond to patrons' time constraints by making sure to ask patrons how quickly they need the information. This helps give the librarians an indication of how time sensitive the inquiry may be and to respond accordingly (see figure 2.2).

FIGURE 2.2   SAMPLE SCREEN FROM DANBURY PUBLIC LIBRARY

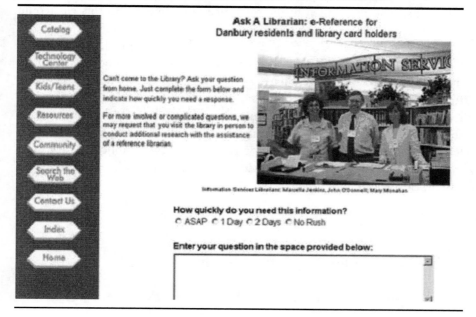

New Directions in Digital Reference

Clearly, changes in the past five years have increased public librarians' ability to provide digital reference services. All digital reference efforts do not build only on the library's Internet presence; more importantly, they also build on the strength of the library's collections and staff. However, as impressive as individual examples are, this service is still in a pioneering stage. Academic libraries have more experience and have more early adopters (Janes et al. 1999). This is not at all surprising since their clientele expect those libraries to provide digital reference. A recent article in *D-Lib Magazine* reflects the urgent need for rapid adoption of this tool. The article reports that "Ask Jeeves, a commercial site that searches the Internet, reports receiving 20 million questions per day and to date has answered more than 150 million questions." However, it notes that a library consortium in northern California tested Ask Jeeves, by sending twelve questions, "no trick questions, none were arcane, just questions typically received by those libraries. Jeeves was unable to answer any of the questions." The inability of a database response system, such as Ask

Jeeves, to answer typical clienteles' questions reveals the need for more librarians, who are skilled in the reference interview, to fill this electronic reference gap.

The Library of Congress is taking the lead in developing the Collaborative Digital Reference Service (CRDS) designed to generate model approaches to providing digital library services, while at the same time harnessing the strength of participating libraries (including major collections such as the Library of Congress) and expert staff (the librarians at the participating institutions around the world). Three public libraries, Santa Monica Public Library, Morris County (NJ) Public Library, and Peninsula (CA) Library System, were among the first wave of collaborators in this grand experiment.

Other Impacts of the Internet on CI

Increased Visibility of CI through the Library's Website

Librarians in our CI survey frequently noted with pride that the Web now makes it possible for CI to be available twenty-four hours a day, seven days a week. By providing prominent access to CI, librarians remind community leaders and citizens that they are experts in providing CI. As a result of CI on the Web, librarians reported increased visibility as well as additional collaboration with service providers and local government. Local government agencies in Multnomah County (OR), New Haven (CT), Darien (CT), and other communities trust the public library staff to maintain their websites (see figure 2.3).

The websites of 295 libraries (71%) included in our director survey not only offer CI developed by the library but also provide links to information developed by others such as local government agencies and nonprofit organizations. This not only increases access to the community's information about itself, but also helps to build community. The best examples of this are seen in our chapters on community networks.

The public libraries of Skokie (IL), http://www.skokie.lib.il.us/ and Hartford (CT) http://www.hartfordpl.lib.ct.us/, as well as many others, prominently link their CI from the top of the library's website. This sends a strong message to the community that the public library is a major player in providing access to CI.

FIGURE 2.3   SAMPLE SCREEN FROM MULTNOMAH PUBLIC LIBRARY

Format Changes—An Overview

The adoption of the Internet as a preferred format for CI is one indication that public library CI providers have made incredible changes in the past five years. We asked CI librarians to indicate the extent to which there had been a change in emphasis in a group of major CI formats in the past five years. On a scale of 1–5 with "1" reflecting no change, 53% of the CI librarians indicated that their library had undertaken major changes ("4" or "5") in the past five years. They reported *more use* of print, the Internet or Web databases, CD-ROM, digitized data, geographic information systems (GIS), OPACs and *less use* of card files and vertical files.

CI reflects the needs of the local community as well as the local library environment. Likewise, change patterns differed practically by year. Thus the range in responses was considerable. Changes included some CI activities that have been eliminated—such as discontinuation of published directories or the elimination of indexing the local newspaper (perhaps because it is now available for purchase from the newspaper). The initial changes reported (those changes up to about 1994) included use of off-the-shelf database software, subscription to databases, and migration of CI from paper files or the card catalog to the OPAC. In 1996 and 1997 changes were likely to be expansion of CI in database format, development of the library's website, migration of CI to the library's new website, the addition of public computer stations that included CI, migration of CI to the OPAC, and engagement in collaborative activities. By 1998–1999 major changes identified by CI librarians included putting CI on the Web, adding digitized local resources—most often photographs and other graphic images. The following comment indicates the changes in one library over time: "1994—migrating CI to OPAC; 1995—migrating CI to Web; 1998—modified search strategies."

Below are a few more comments from respondents that reflect some of the changes:

"Internal database to OPAC"—1994

"Moved to a software that permitted sharing database with community organizations"—1995

"Creation of website for CI"—1996

"Consolidated inaccessible archives of minutes, reports, etc.; cataloged and shelved for independent access rather than staff mediated"—1997

"Digitize photographs of county and issues of local magazine (covering early twentieth century)"—1997

"Migrating print directory and internal database to OPAC"—1998

"100,000 entry local obituary databases made Web accessible"—1999

"Movement of indexing of CI from print source to Web-based indexing as part of Solinet's Community Planet project"—1999

"Limited newspaper indexing"—1999

"Subscription to Orlando Sentinel Online"—1999

The Range of CI Formats

The list of CI formats is considerably longer than it was when libraries began developing CI files. Figure 2.4 titled, "Top Categories and Formats of CI," reflects the nature of change. It shows the staying power of paper as a top format for CI as well as the importance of digital formats for all types of CI. Formats less readily used for CI include kiosks, card files, and vertical files.

FIGURE 2.4   TOP CATEGORIES AND FORMATS OF CI

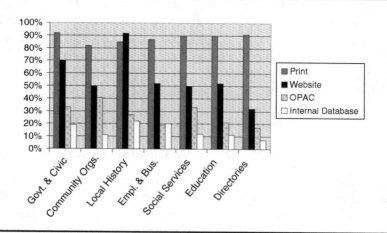

Three-quarters of the libraries reported that their public-access computers (from which citizens can access CI) now have a graphic user interface (Windows or Mac). Overwhelmingly, librarians told us that the
changes they have made have served to increase both the staff's ability to
facilitate the use of CI (91%) and the public's ability to access CI (89%)
(see figures 2.5 and 2.6).

**FIGURE 2.5   STAFF'S ABILITY TO
FACILITATE USE OF CI**

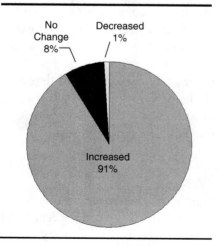

**FIGURE 2.6   PUBLIC'S ACCESS
TO CI**

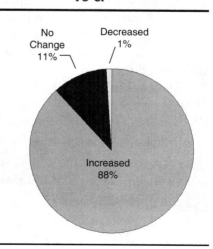

Nearly all CI staff said there was more or much more emphasis on provision of CI on the Web at their library now than five years ago. While we found that CI is available on library websites via both Web-linked, off-the-shelf databases as well as Web-linked OPACs, it appears that increasingly librarians are migrating CI from the OPAC directly to Web-based databases. As we have indicated, putting CI on the Web can mean a logarithmic increase in the public's awareness of it.

Changes in the CI Database Increase Access

The CI file is the cornerstone of CI provision. It was created initially as the basis for public library I&R services (Durrance 1984b; Durrance & Pettigrew 2000). Fifty-four percent of the librarians responding to our CI survey indicated that their library maintained a CI file containing information about social services agencies, local governments, non-profits, and so on.

Traditionally the information in CI files was available only through the mediation of a staff member. In the early 1990s CI databases appeared in greater numbers on OPACs. Baltimore County Public Library continues to feature its CI directory on its CARL Web catalog. More recently many librarians have moved CI to their website and are using off-the-shelf software to link their databases to the Web. These moves have resulted in revolutionary increases in access. A number of librarians indicated that they are exploring even more changes in the CI database with most now determining which software will support their CI database on the Web. Some are considering databases collaboratively developed with other organizations to gain efficiencies of data collection. They also result in an increased awareness among community organizations of librarians' interests, skills, and capabilities.

Our project website features a number of fine examples of database development: http://www.si.umich.edu/libhelp/. (Go to Best Practices and click on Community Information Databases.)

We have sketched several CI-database collaboration projects:

Detroit Public Library TIP Database

Created in 1973, the Detroit Public Library's TIP database was one of the earliest library I&R files in the nation. It continues to provide access to CI by serving as the hub for the Metropolitan Detroit Community Information and Referral Collaborative (MDCIRC), a regional network of I&R programs whose partners include a local United Way, childcare coordinating agencies, and a twenty-four-hour mental health hotline. Recently, the Skillman Foundation awarded a $1.4 million grant to MDCIRC to expand its coverage.

Community Resource Database of Long Island

http://www.crdli.org/

Funded and managed by a coalition of public agencies, private foundations, and businesses, the Community Resource Database of Long Island features more than 8,000 listings for community resources and services. The Middle Country Public Library is the central manager for the database, which is available via public access terminals at libraries and on a subscription basis elsewhere.

San Francisco Community Connection

http://sfpl.lib.ca.us:8000/SOCSER

The San Francisco Public Library's Community Connection provides comprehensive searchable listings of social service agencies, government offices, neighborhood groups, and non-profit organizations. The database is available online at all member libraries via dial-in access and by telephone. The library also offers the AIDS Foundation Database, a separate resource with information on HIV service providers. According to Julie Beach of the Children's Council of San Francisco, "the San Francisco Community Connection is an example of the smart use of the technology that's particularly valuable to non-profit organizations."

Digitization Projects: A New Mechanism to Increase Access and Help Build Community

With their inclusion of digitized data, today's CI databases are much more complex than those from the 1970s and 1980s. Digital collections can enrich an area's cultural tapestry and often reveal for the first time a geographic area's ethnic communities. Working with its African American community, the Public Library of Charlotte-Mecklenburg County (NC) digitized decades of the black experience. The result is *An African American Album: The Black Experience in Charlotte and Mecklenburg County,* which is available on CD-ROM as a library check-out item or for purchase. URL: http://www.cmstory.org/.

By using CARL's digital photographing module, the Los Angeles Public Library (LAPL) provides online access to its extensive collection of historical photos in the LAPL website's Virtual Exhibits section. Contemporary community life in LA's culture-rich ethnic communities is also captured.

A small group of early adopters reported a major increase in providing access to digitized data and included digitization as a CI aspect of which they are very proud. Digitization often starts with historical materials, including photographs from family albums.

Kansas City (MO) Public Library

http://images.kclibrary.org/

"Images of Kansas City" (MO), for example, offers a searchable and browsable collection of historic postcards, maps, biographies, and special exhibits with materials dating back to the 1870s (see figure 2.7).

FIGURE 2.7   SAMPLE SCREEN FROM KANSAS CITY (MO) PUBLIC LIBRARY

Images of Kansas City

Digital Local History Collections from Kansas City Public Library

Photographs
Over 14,000
historical pictures.

Biographies
Biographies of
local historical
figures.

Postcards
As featured in
Kansas City Star
and Times.

Maps *New*
Interactive maps
of historic
Kansas City.

Exhibits
Thematic exhibits
from the digitized
holdings.

Chicago Public Library (CPL)

http://www.chipublib.org/digital/digital.html/

Visitors to the CPL website can explore Chicago's rich traditions by taking one of several narrated virtual tours in their digital collection. Exhibit topics range from Chicago's changing history from pioneer days to African American culture during Chicago's Renaissance to a documentary on the city's urban development. Visitors can discover Chicago then and now through this excellent integration of images and narration.

Tacoma Public Library

http://www.tpl.lib.wa.us/v2/NWRoom/nwroom.htm/

The Tacoma Public Library offers extensive local history material in the Northwest Room area of the website. Here you can view photos from among the library's collection of 1.5 million photographs. The "Unsettling Events" section provides memorable tales of everything from battles to bank frauds and ghost stories to sea monsters. Essays on the region, a ship database, an obituary index, and genealogical information can also be found in these richly filled web pages on the area's history.

Geographic Information Systems (GIS)

The Seattle Public Library (SPL) website helps citizens of that community understand the power of GIS and harness the capability of this software and the data files available through SPL. We are using the SPL message to its citizens about GIS as an introduction to the power of this underutilized tool. Once public librarians acquire the skill to use this tool, their communities will be greatly served. At present GIS is heavily used by businesses and government agencies, but it is still greatly underused by nonprofit organizations, citizen groups, and the general public.

> *Maps:* Create custom maps that display spatial features of interest (themes), using as few or as many themes as desired. The user can view and manipulate geographic information that is stored in the database portion of the GIS. Themes selected by the user will automatically be drawn and displayed on the screen by the GIS software. The GIS public-access workstation at Central Library has a color printer so users can print out the desired maps.

Analysis: Explore relationships between geographic features of interest. Identify patterns and solve everyday problems using advanced techniques of query, selection, analysis, and display.

Reports: Create charts and tables to supplement maps and other documentation. GIS is used at the city to inform decision-makers and planners and to help deliver services to the public. It is available at the Central Library for use by citizens, businesses, neighborhood councils, and other special-interest groups.

We identified some libraries that are currently using GIS. Following are three examples from the project website.

St. Charles City-County Library District

http://www.win.org/library/services/gis/gishp.htm/

The GIS section of the St. Charles City-County (MO) Library District allows citizens to learn about GIS and utilize maps via the Internet. In addition to general information about GIS, including definitions and FAQs, this website contains numerous links to government agencies, international, and commercial websites that offer GIS services. The maps of St. Charles County, Missouri, provide a plethora of data, including information about population distribution by age, race, and income as well as school districts and zip codes.

Enoch Pratt Free Library

http://www.pratt.lib.md.us/info/neighborhoods/

The Enoch Pratt Free Library promotes the use of GIS tools in the Neighborhood Information Resources section of their website. From these pages, community members can compile maps based on demographic and environmental data down to the neighborhood level. These useful pages link to a variety of Internet resources that community groups and citizens can use to plan and map their neighborhoods.

Multnomah County Library

http://www.multnomah.lib.or.us/lib/ref/maps.html/

The Maps/GIS section of Portland's Multnomah County Library website provides links to a variety of regional, national, and international organizations that use GIS software. In addition, the library site hosts Metro, a website with regional government information for Clackamas, Multnomah, and Washington counties. Metro's Natural Hazards project utilizes GIS technology to provide citizens with a variety of maps that illustrate such issues as earthquake hazards, flood inundation, and regional emergency facilities.

Community Information: The Organizational Framework and Staffing

Placement within the Organization

Most libraries (72%) in our detailed study of CI provision indicated that a particular department was responsible for providing CI services. Thirteen percent of the reporting libraries have chosen to separate CI into a separate, most often named, service. However, in most libraries, CI is part of another department. Just more than half of our libraries (51%) indicated that CI is under the auspices of the reference (or information) department. The next, most common placement of the library's CI is in adult or public services (16%). Figure 2.8 presents these data.

FIGURE 2.8   LIBRARY DEPARTMENTS PROVIDING CI

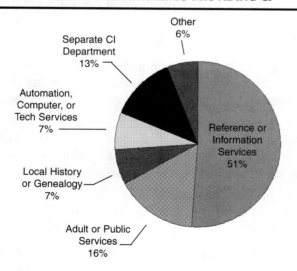

Even within this framework (i.e., reporting to reference or public services) a number of libraries have a special name for the provision of CI. This name is likely to be something very straightforward like "Community Information Services," "Community Information Database" or "Community Information Network." In fact, the most frequent name was some combination of *community* and *information*—with the third word often being *service, project,* or *database.* Naming a service is a message to the community that the library has pulled together materials and provides services to help the community make better use of them. This is in keeping with other named services of public libraries such as Children's Services, Job and Career Center, Local History and Genealogy, and Literacy.

Collection Development and Management

The responsibility to collect and organize CI tends to be shared by several librarians. On average these responsibilities are divided among approximately six staff members. Some libraries also involve volunteers in collecting and organizing CI.

Staffing

No study in decades has attempted to determine the kinds of skills needed by CI staff. We sought to learn the relative value of several types of skills through the following question: "To what extent are any of the following skills needed by library staff who provide CI services today?"

Skills considered essential by our respondents—needed by most or all CI staff—include in rank order: knowledge of the Internet, knowledge of CI resources, knowledge of the reference interview, and ability to train the public.

Skills that CI librarians believe some or most of the staff should have: the ability to communicate the value of CI to library staff, the ability to work with community organizations, and needs-assessment skills.

Skills needed by only a few staff include: the ability to organize CI and needs-assessment skills.

This list indicates that the librarians in our study believe that CI is the responsibility of people with differing skills, inclinations, and abilities, and not everyone needs to know it all.

Librarians were most likely to gain CI ideas and skills from the local library system—73.9% indicating it as a valuable or very valuable resource. Other valuable or very valuable resources for ideas and skills include, in rank order: the state library agency, a state library association, the Public Library Association, a regional library association.

Administrative Support

We sought to determine the strength of support for library CI among administrators and staff. Librarians were most likely (82%) to indicate that they had had very few problems in getting the support they needed for CI from library administrators. Only a few librarians (6%) had difficulty getting the administration to understand their needs. Likewise only a few CI librarians said they had problems getting "buy in" from the staff for library provision of CI. Fifteen percent indicated that they had had some problems with other staff while 6% experienced serious problems, and 79% said that they had encountered no problems with other staff.

Clientele

CI services are more likely to be designed for the general public rather than for a particular clientele. Community networks, on the other hand, often do target special efforts toward non-profit organizations and local government agencies. The chapter on needs and uses of CI indicates the types of CI people look for. The chapter on benefits shows a variety of ways that people benefit from CI. The most common appears to be providing access to CI through CI resources and through answering questions about CI.

The next section reports on what librarians see as the impacts of CI on the way that the library operates in the community. In addition, the chapter on benefits focuses in detail on benefits of CI as identified by citizens, non-profits, local governments, and librarians.

Digital Access, Public Programs, Partnerships, and Other Sources of Staff Pride

We asked CI librarians to identify aspects of providing CI that they were most proud of. Librarians are proud that they have made CI available in digital formats and know that these formats make CI more accessible.

Expanded capabilities of library CI databases make it easier to create customized directories. Librarians are delighted that they have made effective use of the Web and have had a part in digitizing the community's memory. They are proud of public programs that include an array of training opportunities for citizens. Likewise they feel that their work with community organizations has increased library visibility. The increased visibility resulting from these activities has expanded library partnerships, and librarians appear to be proud of the community recognition they have received as a result of their effectiveness in these areas.

Recent years have brought increased Internet-related programming to a number of libraries. Librarians are proud of these services. The public libraries of Saginaw (MI) and Ela (IL) provide training for community groups on how to use electronic CI, while Santa Clara County Library (CA) notes the value of CI-database training. Public libraries that have a strong community networking component, such as the Leon County Public Library's Tallahassee FreeNet, offer courses on building a community networking website and basic and advanced HTML. The needs of specialized social-service providers are met by courses offered by Baltimore County Public Library. Many libraries also offer a full array of information-technology programs for citizens. Through their public programming, CI librarians use the tools of the Internet to communicate with broad segments of the community and to position themselves as knowledge navigators and technology leaders. "The Internet has given us a new set of responsibilities, helping people who have never held a mouse become competent users of the Internet," said one library director.

The Impact of Digital CI and Distributed CI on Access

The process of collecting CI prior to the advent of the Internet was labor-intensive and often frustrating (Durrance 1985). In the pre-Internet era many local governments and non-profit organizations did not see themselves in the information business (so why were those librarians bothering them?)—they were in the service business. Some local governments were even hostile when librarians asked them for copies of documents and reports. The Internet (often with the help of librarians) has actually transformed many local organizations into understanding that they are, indeed, information providers. We have found that local government agencies and community non-profits feel the pressure to make their information available on the Internet. This has begun to transform the way community groups think about librarians—from being seen as nags who focus on collecting and up-dating information into being recognized as experts who show community organizations how to make information accessible.

Information itself is now much more accessible than it was five years ago. Librarians recognize the power of the Internet as a common format both for developers of the information and for its users. The Internet has resulted in information that is more current, more searchable, more comprehensive, involves more formats, and is more interactive (Durrance & Pettigrew 2000).

Librarians enthusiastically indicated that digital information is more usable both to librarians and by the general public. They placed a value in providing the option for people to access CI themselves and in the increased usability of CI in multiple locations, not only throughout the library system, but also throughout the community. Librarians have gone from relying on a single CI file (commented on by several librarians) to the pride of providing CI twenty-four hours a day, seven days a week from multiple locations.

Some CI librarians have found that they actually need less space for an operation, even though the CI is more comprehensive. Increased migration to digital CI has resulted in reducing the amount of vertical file or shelf space previously devoted to paper-formatted CI.

Many CI librarians commented on the impact the changes of the past five years have made both on their own professional practice and on the public's access to CI. We have included some of their comments below.

Accessibility of Information

"CI is now instantly attainable and searchable by need (keyword). Previously our Rolodex could only be searched by staff alphabetically."

"The Library now provides access to WWW for staff and public use at all locations."

"Our statistics indicate that we average 1,000 connections to the Community Resource Database each week, nearly double the statistics from several years ago. We anticipate with more widespread awareness and availability, these numbers to continue to increase."

"It's easier for staff to record agency information changes in the database, and for the new information to be available to the public."

Users Gain Unprecedented Access to Information

"Patrons like to use the computer to retrieve CI."

"Public now [can] use the CI via computer. They no longer have to ask staff about local organizations/support groups, etc."

"Public has more and easier remote access."

"The Inform database, the 'Directory of Clubs and Organizations,' and the Community Information File have allowed patrons to access more information at all library locations."

"Much more CI is available to those people who have home computers with Internet access, and there is more CI available to patrons within the library because the staff has much more access to information than five years ago."

"Web access is making it far easier for all types of users to access our database."

"The new system is available on all OPACs and to remote users; before it was only available on staff terminals. It is also a much more user-friendly team than in the past."

"WWW allows for 24 hr/day access. Local government and school documents are publicly accessible from home now."

Efficiency and Utility

"Development of individual websites by local agencies and organizations helps in accessing current information and cuts down on space requirements in maintaining paper files."

"Staff has much more 'bibliographic control' over the data to find and use it."

"Staff are now able to direct patrons with Internet access at home to the library's website to obtain CI data. In the past patrons had to come in if they were needing a lot of information."

"Staff members now have access to more/better data. Public has improved access, primarily through other human service providers."

Impact of Digital CI on Library-Community Relationships

Digital CI, it appears, not only increases access to needed information, it also can serve to improve communication in the community. It can build bridges among previously unconnected groups. Improved communication can lead to increased library visibility. Increased visibility leads to a recognition by community organizations and citizens that libraries are neutral agencies in the community that are predisposed to bring together all relevant information resources. They also see that librarians are trusted information professionals who know how to increase access to all kinds of information, including information about the local community.

Working together to increase access to digital CI often leads to increased partnerships between libraries and other organizations in the community as well as increased respect for librarians among organizational leaders and citizens.

> "There is increased visibility, marketing, and collaboration with service providers and local government."

> "CI agencies increasingly making information available through the Web and staff are proficient at finding it or referring patrons to it."

> "Our partnership with United Way has increased community and library's access and ability to use of CI, tremendously. Previously, the information was gathered, maintained, and accessed through a system located in another county."

> "We have had more cooperation with local government as a result of the Web."

Building Community through Partnerships

Building partnerships with other organizations is a basic cornerstone to building community. A broad spectrum of community partnerships by CI librarians has been commonplace since the CI revolution of the 1970s. Now that librarians expertly provide CI using the Internet, both their credibility and the value of the public library in the community has increased. Librarians in our study noted that the benefits of collaboration accrue to the library, the agencies, and to the community. Figure 2.9 shows that collaboration is a win-win activity.

We were told by many that library partnerships have resulted in an increased awareness in the community of the value of the library, additional collaboration opportunities, increased responsibilities in community partnerships, more public support for library millages, and awards for excellence.

The New Haven (CT) Free Public Library (NHFPL), for example, is one of several designated partners in the city's Empowerment Zone; others

FIGURE 2.9   IMPACT OF COLLABORATION

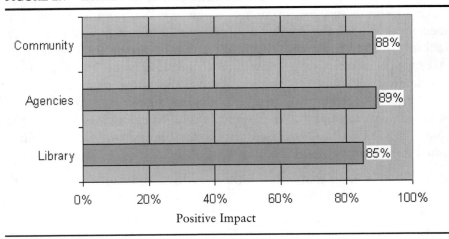

include the city, selected non-profit organizations, and Yale University. Library Hotline indicates that this is the first time that a public library has participated in an Empowerment Zone technology plan (Sept. 6, 1999). City Librarian Howard McGinn told us that NHFPL is seen as a major locus of information technology expertise for the city. The library's track record as a trusted institutional partner in the community certainly set the stage for the collaboration. Furthermore, staff leadership in providing expertise in Internet technologies positioned the library for this and other community collaborations including one recently started with the New Haven Police Department and the U.S. Department of Justice to bring community GIS data to citizens.

Impacts of Collaboration on the Library

Librarians frequently noted that as a result of their collaborative activities, community organizations that had not previously known of the library's community roles had become library supporters. They frequently commented that collaboration resulted in involvement in additional community projects. With additional community involvement comes increased respect from other community organizations. One library noted that they had recently won the Chamber of Commerce Technology Leadership

Award as a result of their collaborative activities. Several pointed out that they were convinced that the library building referendum passed easily at least in part as a result of the community support generated by collaborative activities.

Impacts of Collaboration on Partner Agencies and the Community

Librarians' reports on the impacts of collaboration on partner agencies centered on the limited community funds available to non-profit organizations and the importance of being good stewards of public money. They point out that collaboration reduces redundancy of services. Non-profits, librarians told us, benefit from the neutral image of the library. Non-profits are able to use the library's facilities, thus saving their resources for other purposes. Collaboration with community organizations gives librarians an insider's view of the organization. Collaboration results in joint ventures (public training, collaborative purchasing, staff development workshops, marketing) that benefit both parties. And of course, collaboration increases communication. Reaching out to community organizations benefits the broader community represented by these groups. "Our work with the Asian community has brought their attention to the library and assisted us in providing materials in Asian languages."

Visibility on the Web

In sum, library Internet access has had considerable effects on the provision of CI. Initially CI was primarily an outreach service, carried out through the use of paper files or internal databases. Public library use of the Internet has resulted in a Web presence, which means much greater external visibility. The Web has provided public librarians with a tool for a number of innovative approaches including, in many libraries, digital reference capability, databases that more easily interface with the Internet, impressive examples of digitization of CI, and in a few libraries, experiments with powerful tools such as GIS. Some libraries have taken advantage of the power of the library's website to give a considerably higher CI profile. Many have adopted a wide variety of formats for displaying CI. These activities have resulted in positive impacts on citizens and organizations and in an increased ability to engage in partnerships with other community organizations, an increased ability to meet users' needs, and the opportunity to work with others to build community. These gains have brought cachet to many libraries in an increased understanding by community leaders and citizens of the value of public libraries in building community.

3

Public Library Participation in Community Networking

This chapter and chapter 4 on benefits together answer the questions: "How do public libraries participate in community networking, and how do librarians expect participation will help clients and benefit communities?" We describe participation in community networking in detail, first by defining and describing the community-networking phenomenon and then by examining library participation. The next chapter continues this examination by focusing on the benefits of community networks to individuals, community organizations, the larger community, and to public libraries themselves.

Community Networking Overview

The Community Networking Phenomenon: "A Community Network is a locally based, locally driven communication and information system designed to enhance community and enrich lives."

The emergence of the personal computer, standardized operating systems, affordable modems, low-cost telecommunications software for host computers as well as end-users, cheap disk space and memory, combined with the political restlessness following the 1960s, provided ideal ingredients for the rise of community networks (CNs) (Durrance & Schneider 1996). New societal and institutional responses such as CNs arise when the conditions are right. Over a hundred years ago a constellation of conditions made the development of the free public library feasible, economical, and socially valuable. In the past century, it has become a valued institution in the community.

The first "community network" is thought to be Community Memory, a network based in Berkeley in the 1970s that deployed several terminals in a store, a laundromat, and a community center (Cisler 1994; Schuler 1996). A decade later as the result of a more mature computing environment, an interactive, community-based bulletin-board system at Case Western Reserve University in Cleveland spawned the nation's first "free-net," the Cleveland Free-Net, and a number of other free-nets in the next decade (Durrance & Schneider 1996). Free-nets initially used ASCII text and bulletin-board software; they provided free email accounts for thousands of individuals and fostered the initial excitement about CNs.

By the early 1990s, as CNs began to adopt Web technologies, they were seen as having the potential for making major social changes in their communities. Philanthropist Mario Morino speaking at one of the early community networking conferences in 1994, said:

> The local community is where our toughest social problems—crime, inadequate education, underemployment—will be solved, by the grass-roots efforts of the people who have the most personal stake in their solution. It is here that community networking takes on such relevance in helping people solve problems and addressing the needs of their day-to-day lives. Clearly, community networking is an emerging phenomenon with the potential to effect profound societal transformation (Morino 1994).

By the mid-1990s major funders, including several governmental agencies and foundations, made major investments in the CNs in a number of geographic areas, and these organizations began to use the common term "community networks." Leaders brought together hundreds who were involved in CNs to several national conferences and developed a national association devoted to CNs, the Association for Community Networking (ACN). These activities coincided with the introduction of the Web to wider audiences and resulted in the Web generation of CNs that harnessed the power of the Internet for local communities. The Web generation of CNs with public library involvement is the innovation that the majority of public libraries embraced and thus is the subject of our IMLS-sponsored research. Although the term "free-net" is still used by some library early adopters of the phenomenon such as Tallahassee FreeNet, SEFLIN Free-Net, and Three Rivers Free-Net, they all refer to themselves as CNs.

While CNs made meteoric gains during the rapid development of the Web in the mid-1990s, countervailing forces were also at work. Commercial ventures such as Microsoft Sidewalk developed CN-like presences in a number of communities with the idea that there might be a reasonable return on their investment (only to find near the end of the decade that there was no money to be made in this venture). Likewise, the adoption of the Internet by government agencies and other institutions sometimes slowed, rather than accelerated, the pace of CN development. By 1997 the major concern among CNs was sustainability.

As a result, some notable CNs, including the pioneering Cleveland Free-Net and several of its sister free-nets, have vanished or are greatly diminished most often because they failed to gain on-going support from the community. However, CNs with strong ties to existing community institutions such as the public library are viable, robust, community-building vehicles. It is far too soon to write the obituary for the community networking movement. Its potential as a community-building tool is far too great. The challenge facing CNs will be to assure that primary community partners, funders, and supporters—existing institutions in the community like public libraries—continue to support this phenomenon. This study examines the extent and nature of that support by public library systems.

How Public Libraries and Librarians Participate in CNs: An Extension of Previous Roles

For more than a decade a group of best practice libraries have played pivotal roles in CN development. CNs provide citizens with equitable access to the Internet for obtaining CI and communicating with others; they provide citizens with one-stop shopping for access to governmental, social services, local information, email, and Internet access. CI is a central CN feature that appears in many forms: I&R agencies and libraries, for example, may mount their databases on the Internet, while individual service providers may post information about their programs and services. Thus, the architecture of the Internet makes networked CI possible by linking information files created not only by single organizations such as libraries, but also by agencies, organizations, and individuals throughout the community. This is a major departure from traditional I&R services where librarians and other CI-agency staff work with files about the community that are created on an internal library system.

As discussed in the last chapter, public libraries are more likely to provide digital CI than they are to engage in the more intensive activity, involvement in building a CN. Providing digital CI does not require the extensive commitment of time and resources devoted to CNs. (Likewise, the benefits to the library may be less noticeable.) Nonetheless, public libraries are powerful contributors to community networking both in their communities and as participants in the national and international community networking activities.

Public library leaders involved in CNs see this as a vital role for public libraries and librarians. Sarah Long, 1999–2000 president of the American Library Association and the vision behind NorthStarNet, told us:

> The reason that it seemed to me that something like NorthStarNet was a good idea is because this is a business that public libraries have always been in. . . . To collect community information. The library should be the place to find out who's the president of the PTA and so on and so forth. . . . The computer made keeping this information much more feasible—keeping it up to date and being more pervasive.

Our study of public library CNs shows how libraries participate in CNs; we have identified best practice in library-developed CNs. We found a wide range of public library involvement with CNs due to the local nature of the phenomenon and the variation in approaches taken by libraries. This chapter examines best practice and its implications. CNs have the potential to model ways to build virtual community; they can increase the skills of community leaders; and they can position librarians for a leadership role in bringing information technology to the community. CNs associated with public libraries appear to be mechanisms that help librarians work more effectively with non-profit organizations, local governments, and other partners.

CN Models and Activity Range: The Data

There is no definitive census of CNs; however, patterns appear that, unlike public libraries, have not yet been developed in most communities. Because of its importance to our study of the provision of CI in the digital age, we examined community networking both in our initial survey of public library directors and in our focused survey of providers of CI. Fourteen percent of the directors (N = 71) said that their library was currently involved in a CN. Our 1999 survey of CI coordinators provided us with additional information about the ways that public libraries are involved in CNs (see table 3.1). Thirty-one libraries indicated their year of initial CN involvement. On average they had been involved for four and a half years with some going back to the early 1990s, the free-net era.

Our research showed a mean of 2.29 staff members engaged in the community networking enterprise. CN staff members (some full time, some part time) are engaged in a variety of activities. The types of contributions that public libraries and librarians are most likely to make to CNs include providing the server for the CN, terminals so that citizens can access the CN, providing content for the CN, developing and hosting web pages, providing training, and making the library's meeting room available for community networking meetings. Librarians may also work with volunteers who assist in CN development, participate in policymaking, host CN training and meetings, provide funding, involve staff in CN governance, or provide programming.

Table 3.2, in rank order, reflects the range of library involvement in CNs based on our national survey.

Table 3.1   Average Number of Years of Library Involvement with Community Networks

Year	Average Number of Years Libraries Have Been Involved with Community Network
1999	1 (3.2% of total)
1998	4 (12.9% of total)
1997	4 (12.9% of total)
1996	6 (19.4% of total)
1995	9 (29.0% of total)
1994	3 (9.7% of total)
1993 or earlier	4 (12.9% of total)

N = 31; mean 4.5 years

Table 3.2   The Extent of Library Involvement in Community Networks

Types of CN Support	Major	Rank
Provide server for CN	65.2% (15/23)	1
Provide terminals for CN	58.3% (14/24)	2
Provide content	58.3% (14/24)	2
Develop web pages	56.5% (13/23)	3
Host web pages	55.0% (11/20)	4
Provide training	45.5% (10/22)	5
Provide meeting room	42.9% (9/21)	6
Work with volunteers	40.9% (9/22)	7
CN policy making (posting, proper use)	40.0% (8/20)	8
Funding	36.4% (8/22)	9
Host training	33.3% (7/21)	10
Governance	33.3% (6/18)	10
Host meetings	31.8% (7/22)	11
Provide programming	27.8% (5/18)	12

Statistics provide an overview of CN components, but only begin to scratch the surface. The value and potential impact of library involvement in community networking can be seen far more clearly by examining these community institutions. The Help Seek project website identifies a number of public library–CN initiatives. The models of involvement vary with the community. Each community has a different set of needs and circumstances. To provide a better sense for what a CN does and how it works, we have included a few CN examples below. They show the range of activities and suggest the benefits that accrue both to the community and to the library, which is seen as a leader in networking a community. Following these short examples are quotes from community networking leaders interviewed as part of our case study research. These quotes reflect what leaders see as the role of public library participation in community networking. Our three case-study CNs, profiled later in this chapter, provide the rich detail that enriches our knowledge of participation in community networking.

Community Network Examples

Across the U.S. and Canada there is a pattern of public library involvement with CNs. The Canadian Library Association and the American Library Association have held sessions that focus on CNs as a phenomenon. Public libraries can and do participate in the ACN. We have selected four CNs from a number featured on our project website under the heading: Public Library--CN Initiatives. These four provide an introduction to our rich description of public library community networking involvement.

These four public library–CN initiatives reflect the leadership taken by these public libraries in increasing access to the community's information about itself. These projects virtually depict the community with information by and about local non-profits and other organizations, health and social-services agencies, libraries, museums and educational institutions, some businesses and employers, and local and state governments. By bringing all this information (created by a number of organizations including, but not limited to, the library) together in one place the library adds considerable value to it. They provide one-stop shopping for CI. Some also help the community keep track of its events by creating, hosting, or linking to a community calendar. Some add value to information by investing in information infrastructure for the good of the community—a server, software, tech support, and so on. They add value by modeling collaboration among organizations and training community leaders in technology use. Finally, to paraphrase one of the CNs below, these CNs can function as catalysts for educational, social, and economic growth in their communities.

Danbury Community Network

http://www.danbury.org/

The Danbury (CT) Community Network was established in 1995 and is maintained by the Danbury Public Library and local volunteers. The website provides a folksy charm with a historic photograph of the community taken sometime in the 1930s. Six buttons clearly present the types of information available through this network: information and events, community (including clubs and organizations), health and social-services organizations, education and libraries (including area public and private schools and colleges), government (which focuses on local and state governments in Connecticut), and business (which includes organizations of businesses in the area). Those who go to the CN's website are encouraged to: "Discover links to the people, organizations, and information which make the greater Danbury Connecticut community a great place to live, work and play." When visitors explore these pages, they will find information about training programs, an area calendar of events, area media, parks, transportation, religious organizations, and so on.

Milford Community Information Network

http://milford.lib.mi.us/MCIN/comm.htm/

Michigan's Milford Township Library "is dedicated to linking Milford Area residents, local government, business, healthcare, education, human services, and cultural organizations to each other and to the rest of the world." This public library is committed to fulfilling its mission to meet the educational, informational, recreational, and cultural needs of area residents, and in doing so has created the Milford Community Information Network (MCIN). MCIN provides valuable local data and provides free introductory Internet training. Its CI is divided into grouped content under logical headings that include arts and culture, clubs and organizations, community development, education, environment, government, health, human services, libraries, religion, sports, and youth and family.

The user of the CN is also encouraged to find out about the Milford area by viewing village and township history as well as area maps. The site also links information about the larger geographic area.

Darien Community Information Network

http://darien.lib.ct.us/

The Darien CI Network is a notable example of the role that a library can play in the creation of a small town's information infrastructure. The library hosts the websites for town-related organizations, such as the town hall, schools, the library, and non-profit organizations. For a town with a population of roughly 18,000, the CN provides an extensive directory of non-profit organizations. Local churches link their web pages alongside civic associations, political groups, and social-service agencies, reflecting Darien's diverse non-profit community. In addition, the CN features a community calendar, which lists a range of events, such as health seminars, concerts, zoning meetings, and book talks. The library's position as the central CI provider for Darien has drawn increased attention to the library. According to Louise Berry, director of the Darien Public Library, "the library has received increased financial and political support as a result of taking the leadership role in technology for the town." Darien stands as an example of how a small town library's electronic innovations better serve the community, while highlighting the unique role of the library as the CI provider (see figure 3.1).

The Tallahassee Freenet

http://www.tfn.net/

The Tallahassee Freenet (TFN), Florida's first CN and one of the nation's first library–CN partnerships, was started in 1993 by faculty from Florida State University (FSU). Early on, the LeRoy Collins Leon County Public Library joined as an operating partner. Over time partners have changed, but the public library has continued to be a primary stakeholder. TFN has ties to county government, state government, area universities, the newspaper, hospitals, and hundreds of community organizations. TFN seeks to serve as "a catalyst for the educational, social, and economic growth of Tallahassee, Leon County, and Florida through online community networking." They do this by involving community businesses and individuals as supporters, partners, and volunteers who serve in a variety of capacities including acting as editors of content web pages.

FIGURE 3.1   SAMPLE SCREEN FROM DARIEN COMMUNITY INFORMATION NETWORK

Information about the town, schools, organizations and businesses of Darien, Connecticut

The Public Library Community
Network Model: The Case Study Data

Selecting the Community Networks

The aim of the case-study portion of the project was to identify and study best practice associated with public library–community networking initiatives. Therefore we sought to identify those CNs most likely to exhibit "best practice." Our case-study communities, then, were identified from nationally known CNs with major public library participation. Since 1994, the University of Michigan School of Information has maintained a major site focusing on CNs, the Community Connector, http://www.si. umich.edu/Community/. It was used in the initial filtering process. We identified library–CN initiatives with strong CI content. In addition, we sought CNs that had received national recognition such as a nomination or award from the Global Information Infrastructure program of the U.S. Department of Commerce National Telecommunications and Information Administration Telecommunications and Information Infrastructure Assistance Program, now known as the Technology Opportunities Program.

Data Collection Approaches

During the case-study phase of the research, we traveled to the three chosen communities (Pittsburgh, PA; suburban Chicago, IL; and Portland, OR) in order to gain in-depth data on how libraries participate in community networking initiatives, and more importantly, what differences these initiatives make in the community. We communicated not only with those who are responsible for the CN design and operation and administrators of the parent library organization, but also with community non-profit organizations, local human-service providers, and local government agencies. Lastly, we involved users of these CNs in our study, focusing on not only their use of the CN but also their information behavior while searching for CI on the Internet. We gained rich data from all that were involved. Those data are discussed throughout this final study and have been distilled into the case-study summaries that appear below.

The detailed profiles of the Three Rivers Free-Net (TRFN) (Carnegie Library of Pittsburgh), NorthStarNet (NSN) (North Suburban Library System and Suburban Library System), and CascadeLink (Multnomah County Public Library) synthesize the models we identified from our site visits. These case studies and a number of live links to additional community resources and features are also available on the project website, http://www.si.umich.edu/libhelp/. They provide detail about how each public library system developed a distinct CN model appropriate for its community. Our examination of these three library-supported CNs has strongly contributed to the benefits section that follows these descriptions.

Common Approaches Used by Case Study Community Networks

The three case-study CNs profiled below have in common some elements or approaches. Each CN reflects the *mission* of its parent organization, and, just as importantly, the *knowledge, skills,* and *values* of librarians. The leadership in these best practice CNs are able to *assess situations* and local conditions. In addition, each CN model seeks to solve a local-access *problem* or to improve existing access. The actual CN model developed will result from a variety of *community and library circumstances* and consist of a range of content development and service considerations. Leaders of these three CNs recognize the need to provide *training and technical assistance* to community organizations and non-profit groups—how they do it varies. They are likely to *convene* or otherwise bring community organizations together (through Web technology, electronic discussion lists, etc.). They find different ways to show community groups the value of linking to related organizations. CN leaders *foster communication* among community organizations. They know that communication leads to the creation of new *partnerships* among community groups. The CN is a mechanism for *modeling* activities that result in increased collaboration, volunteerism, training, and other benefits to the community. These common approaches are illustrated below. Some include quotes from the cadre of CN leaders we interviewed (including CN staff and library administrators).

Mission or Aim

These three CNs grow out of the parent public library's commitments to provide information and increase access to information. The aims of these three networks are similar—to increase access to community resources. TRFN, for example, seeks to facilitate "the collection, organization, and dissemination of Pittsburgh regional information in a public space." NSN is designed to help bring Chicago's suburban communities together in virtual space even though they are dispersed in physical space. By linking together 124 communities, NSN seeks to help make life in Chicago's suburbs more cohesive.

The CN reflects librarians' knowledge, skills and values.

"One of the benefits of being part of the library is that we, our constituency, are everyone. No one is left out. We represent all points of view. Neutral content. You know, no one. We don't have clients that we have to cater to. We treat everyone equally, so it's a very safe place to be."

"One thing I say all the time—that the library is information neutral. It can represent the entire community. Any other organization couldn't be that way. We even link to the man [who is] trying to close government down."

CN librarians are aware of local conditions.

The leaders of the three CNs are aware of local conditions, start where the community is, and bring them along. In the process they develop resources that are needed by the community. These resources from all three CNs included community non-profit organizations and local government agencies.

Model development depends on community and library conditions.

This means that each of these three CNs looks different, but each represents the needs and resources of the local community. NSN is a distributed model that is designed to respond to the needs of many communities and libraries. The genius of this model is that the community knows a local CN like SkokieNet by its community name, but the name also alerts the community to its linkages to the larger CN—NSN. The other two are more centralized models also based on the nature of their parent organizations.

Each CN seeks to overcome problems associated with the community that hinder community building. TRFN seeks to overcome the problems associated with splintered community resulting from the area's scenic mountains and rivers. NSN seeks to overcome suburban sprawl. CascadeLink seeks to help keep the Portland area a thriving urban community.

Librarians provide assistance to non-profit organizations and local governments.

This assistance varies depending on the model. All CNs helped their non-profit organizations and local government agencies learn how to become information providers and how to gain visibility through developing a website. At NSN much of this work is distributed through the local member libraries.

CN leaders bring CI providers together.

CN leaders recognize that other organizations in the community have information and resources to contribute to the CN. They also recognize that citizens need and benefit from information from a variety of community resources. "I talk about the homeless problem and finding resources for the homeless. You should be able to find a food bank and they should get you to shelters and vice versa. You shouldn't have to go back to square one again and start your search again."

CN librarians show non-profits how to link to other organizations.

Community group leaders in all three case-study communities told us that the CN taught them the importance of linking to other, related organizations. One librarian said: "I talk about the baby website and the importance of getting your information out, but also of linking to complementary or next-step services or categories in your areas. You already have people that you collaborate with. Why not link to them on your website? Get your people thinking, if I am at Mom's House. Well, I'll use my typical example, Zor Home is a residential treatment facility for addicted women with children and so once they have gone through that program, it just makes sense that they might want to think about going back to school and so they would need day care or parenting classes, which are two things that Mom's House provides. So why not have Zor Home point to organizations like Mom's House?"

CN fosters communication.

CN librarians foster communication and collaboration and involve community organizations in developing the CN. This may involve convening community organizations and groups with very positive results. It may also involve the use of electronic discussion lists and the web site as communication mechanisms.

CN *staff foster partnerships.*

"I was just talking to the director of [a Southern library]. They are getting ready [to] start a CI network in [their community]. The thing I was telling her was that I thought that they needed to get the police department or the social services, the park district on board. She said to me that they had actually already formed a committee that consists of these kinds of people. I think that is going to go a long way to building a successful project, and it's not seen as something the library is pushing or something the library is doing alone."

CN *staff model community building.*

Librarians use their expertise to model community building through the Web. In each of the three communities, community non-profit leaders were extremely impressed by the librarians' abilities to organize CI.

"I think the thing that was most interesting to me in [our CN public meeting a few weeks ago] was that I was sitting there in a room with people representing pretty much every facet of a community. . . . I think our library's responsibilities need to be more in fostering that sense of community—helping people make connections. The library knows who the police person is, and they know who the PTA president is. They are the ones that can put those people together online or in person. NSN, again, by using that as a tool for getting people into the library a couple times a year, suddenly the PTA president and the police chief are in the same room together. Maybe that's never happened before in that town. Maybe they have something to say to each other on how they can do some programs and work together."

The public library leads collaborative community efforts.

CN leaders see the need for collaborative efforts and often take the lead in fostering them. NSN's challenge is to foster collaboration not only across communities but also among librarians in these differing communities. CascadeLink fosters collaboration among local government agencies who act as stakeholders in the CN.

The CN fosters volunteerism.

This is done in various ways. Volunteers help build CN content. The CNs also are vehicles for identifying volunteering opportunities in the communities they serve.

Librarians know that the CN brings direct benefits to their communities.
Each of the three indicated getting feedback from the community
regarding community-building activities that result because of the
CN. Our chapter on benefits details how CNs bring broad benefits to their communities.

Ginnie Cooper, director of the Multnomah County Public
Library, captures an overarching value to the CN—that it
increases the community's access to information and thus its
resources. "It is important to make sure that that information is
available to the community. And when I say that information, I
mean from a variety of different sources, the library's only one of
them. That's more important than that people know that this is a
library program."

CASE STUDY 1

Three Rivers Free-Net: Free to the People

http://trfn.clpgh.org/

"Free to the People" is something of a mantra for the librarians at the
Carnegie Library of Pittsburgh (CLP). This phrase, originally spoken by
Andrew Carnegie, the library's founder, is the first thing you see as you
approach the stone facade of CLP's main branch. The ideals of community, public service, and access that the words imply are ones that all
public librarians strive to achieve. Therefore, it is hardly surprising that
the Three Rivers Free-Net (TRFN), an electronic CN funded by the CLP,
housed at the main library, and run by librarians would take these words
to heart (see the screen logo at figure 3.2). In August of 1999, our research
team visited TRFN and talked with its staff members as well as its library
and community partners. In that time, Carnegie's words came up repeatedly, spoken by librarians, TRFN staff, and members of non-profit
groups. One non-profit staffer citing Carnegie, stated matter-of-factly,
"The 'free' part of the Free-Net is important." TRFN represents a powerful model of a CN built upon public library principles. What follows are
our team's impressions of this noteworthy library–CN partnership.

History and Philosophy

The Free-Net was born in the mid-1990s through a grant awarded to the CLP. Today, TRFN is funded entirely through the CLP's budget, which pays the salaries of three on-site staff members as well as a part-time systems administrator who works off-site. Susan Holmes, the project manager for TRFN, has been a librarian for a number of years and uses the skills for organization and community building that she honed on the library floor. Maureen Pollard, TRFN's CN specialist, oversees training initiatives. Meanwhile, Automation Librarian Cathy Chaparro is responsible for maintaining TRFN's Subject Guide and addressing technical issues.

On the website, TRFN's mission is described as facilitating "the collection, organization and dissemination of Pittsburgh regional information in a public space." Its constituents include any potential user of the site in southwestern Pennsylvania, as well as all locally based non-profit and governmental agencies. TRFN serves the population at large in many ways, perhaps most importantly by providing access to information on thousands of regional (as well as valuable national and international) non-profit organizations. Likewise, TRFN serves local agencies by making it easier for the public, volunteers, and funders to find information about them. TRFN does this by carefully organizing links to resources on its website and by offering server space and website training to non-profit organizations. Many of TRFN's services are provided at no cost.

FIGURE 3.2   SAMPLE SCREEN OF LOGO FROM THREE RIVERS FREE-NET

An Alternate Geography

When Pittsburgh residents describe their home, the term "provincial" is likely to come up. In this, Pittsburgh is a product of its geography. Many of the characteristics that make Pittsburgh a scenic place—its three rivers, its many neighborhoods built upon rolling hills—are also those that tend to separate municipalities from each other. This results in a patchwork of towns and boroughs that oftentimes do not communicate well with each other or collaborate on programs. In fact, there are 130 municipalities in Allegheny County—TRFN's home county—alone. Ironically, despite (or perhaps because of) the tendency towards "provincialism," the non-profit network in Pittsburgh is extensive—there are more than 3,000 health and human-service organizations in the area—and tightly knit. Area non-profits are very much interested in working together to solve problems, and TRFN works to build connections between Pittsburgh's many dispersed resources so that they can make things happen.

Author Paul Bowles once wrote that "the only effort worth making is the one it takes to learn the geography of one's own nature." In a sense, by working to link in cyberspace non-profits that don't easily meet in real space, TRFN does just that; it creates an internal geography to counter Pittsburgh's segmented physical geography. In this goal, TRFN is supported by its relationship with the Electronic Information Network for Public Libraries in Allegheny County (eiNetwork), which is working to build an "electronic network [that] will provide libraries in the county with cost-effective access to an electronic tool that enhances library planning, management, communication, and resource building and creates an electronically integrated library system."

TRFN builds a virtual community in part through the thoughtful construction of its website. When you give a passing glance to the TRFN subject guide (see figure 3.3), which outlines the structure of the site, you see an arrangement quite similar to Yahoo!'s homepage or the hundreds of Yahoo! copyists on the Internet.

However, upon closer examination you find that, instead of the somewhat haphazard structure of Yahoo!, TRFN is built with a librarian's eye for organization. The site is divided into twenty carefully considered subject areas, ranging from cultural activities to employment to social services. These, in turn, lead to more detailed subcategories and, ultimately, to specific resources in the Pittsburgh area and elsewhere. Organizations that can fit under more than one category are cross-referenced to give

FIGURE 3.3   SAMPLE SCREEN FROM THREE RIVERS FREE-NET

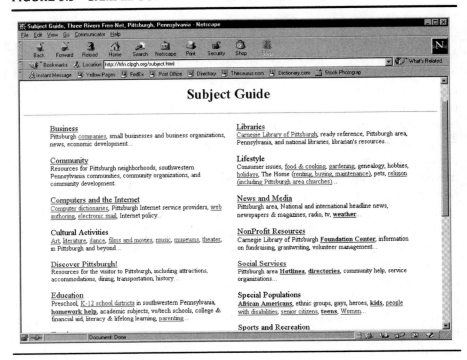

users as many logical points of access as possible. Not only does this make it easier for TRFN users to find what they are looking for, it also helps unify Pittsburgh's non-profit community. Groups interested in, say, adoption can find like-minded groups categorized on the same page. In addition, agencies who have yet to build a presence on the Internet can look to TRFN's subject pages for inspiration.

Raising Awareness

While providing access to agency information for the Pittsburgh community is an impressive accomplishment in itself, the staff at TRFN feels that serving as a passive portal to these resources is insufficient. Their definition of "access" is more broad. It requires that TRFN take active steps to assure non-profit and government agencies are able to reach out to the community. Because they recognize that many non-profit organizations operate on a shoestring and are therefore not likely to have a surplus of resources (funds and staff) to devote to creating web pages, TRFN hosts agency pages on its own server. This is no small commitment. Not only does TRFN provide non-profits (which the free-net staff refer to as "information providers," or IPs) with server space and one free email account per group, they also offer training classes on setting up an effective page, using HTML and email, and more. Because many non-profit agencies don't have access to the latest equipment or technical advice, this level of training is essential to TRFN's mission. The trainers at TRFN receive consistently high marks from the IPs they serve.

IPs are required to participate in an account class, which covers how to connect with TRFN, basic UNIX commands, text editing, email, and file transfer protocol. A second optional course focuses on HTML. In addition, TRFN offers an open lab where IPs can work on the content and design of their pages and turn to TRFN staff members as needed for advice and technical assistance. While teaching is the primary order of the day for TRFN's trainers, they also take the sessions as an opportunity to do some low-key "preaching" as well. For example, oftentimes agency staff who attend the classes are not entirely sold on the idea of a web page. (They may have been "sent" by an enthusiastic board member.) In these situations, the trainers work to sell the notion of a site as a means of local, state, national, and international exposure. In addition, trainers encourage new IPs to link with related agencies—with an emphasis on those in southwestern Pennsylvania—both to serve users and to support sister organizations. Because non-profit groups are in the business of helping people, this idea is readily embraced. As one non-profit staff member put it, "In the non-profit community, we want to help each other out, so we should provide links to related organizations whenever appropriate."

New software on the horizon will allow non-profits to easily build their own websites with much less training. At that point, the challenge to TRFN staff will be how to continue to instill in community non-profits that the success of virtual community lies at least in part in the links that non-profits themselves make to other IPs. In other words, while TRFN's teaching role may lessen over time, the "preaching" component will still be needed.

Lists, a Vehicle for Community Building

TRFN uses electronic discussion lists as another method of building relationships between IPs. All IPs are required to sign up for the IP electronic discussion list, which the free-net describes as a tool that "enables the

TRFN staff to communicate with ALL of the TRFN Information Providers and for the Information Providers to ask questions of us and each other." In addition, IPs are encouraged to participate in the Nonprofit Organizations Mailing List, which is intended to "promote the flow of information among southwestern Pennsylvania non-profit organizations." Meanwhile, the TRFN technical issues list is "dedicated to the discussion of technical issues related to TRFN . . . among interested TRFN Information Providers, TRFN volunteers, and TRFN staff."

Success Stories

During our Pittsburgh visit, we spoke with a variety of IPs and many explained how their collaboration with TRFN strengthened their organization and assisted their clientele. A common thread that ran through many of the stories we heard was the impact of technology. Technology was never described as an end in itself but rather as a means of reaching out to the community. Here are a handful of success stories:

> The Allegheny County Health Department (ACHD) is a newcomer to TRFN. Its site provides information on health topics— from Air Quality to Workplace Hazards—that are of interest to the region. County risk levels and prevention methods are discussed, agency plans for addressing problems are considered, and links to related resources are provided. In our interview with Mary Jones and Dave Piposar from ACHD, they praised TRFN's efforts—in conjunction with eiNetwork—to make information accessible to underserved communities via library computers: "TRFN is the single greatest opportunity of access for minorities." In addition, they noted the health department's partnership with the free-net was a natural because "neither is out to make a profit or take advantage, and both are there to bring more information to the community."

> Dave Noble is the director of the Radio Information Service (RIS), which broadcasts readings from newspapers, magazines, and books for the visually impaired. While RIS currently broadcasts over FM radio, they have started to make their programs available on demand via Real Audio streaming on their TRFN web page. Noble sees this technology as a way to give "blind drivers a lane

on the information superhighway." TRFN also serves RIS' clientele by requiring that all of its web pages are designed to be easily accessible for the visually impaired.

Mike Bookser, the chief of the Bellevue Police Department, feels that TRFN is a tool for making government more responsive and approachable. He hopes that, by giving people the opportunity to interact with the department anonymously online, they will be more likely to turn to it for answers. Bookser also praised TRFN's trainers for tailoring a training session to suit his experience. His experiences with the free-net have been so positive that he encouraged other organizations—including the Borough of Bellevue, St. Cyril School, and Mothers Against Drunk Driving—to sign up as IPs.

The Three Rivers Center for Independent Living (TRCIL) strives to "empower people with disabilities to live self-directed, productive, and personally meaningful lives in a self-determined setting." Leila Rao of TRCIL was particularly proud of the online version of the Access Guide to Pittsburgh, which appears on their TRFN-sponsored page. The guide offers information on access to parking, buildings, restrooms, telephones, water fountains, etc., provided by local businesses to persons with disabilities. Rao also noted that funding was offered to her organization by a foundation that "discovered" TRCIL's web page on TRFN.

Additional success stories are accessible via the TRFN website.

Shared Characteristics of the Community Network and the Public Library

As paradoxical as it seems, the aspects of TRFN that make it distinctive in the world of electronic community networking are the ones that it shares in common with its counterpart in the brick-and-mortar world: the public library. While the profile above mentioned several characteristics that libraries share with TRFN, a few bear repeating:

Both have a local focus while still linking to the larger world.

Both, true to Andrew Carnegie's wishes, offer most of their services free of charge. Their decisions are not colored by a profit motive.

The Free-Net and public libraries both have traditions of public service. Each is dedicated to reaching out to underserved groups. Access is of paramount importance.

Libraries impact the lives of all community residents in manifold ways. As Herb Elish, the director of the Carnegie Library, puts it, "Everyone has a library story." TRFN is an important part of that story in Pittsburgh. Other noteworthy community-building programs offered by the library include its Foundation Center and Job and Career Education Center. For more information on the TRFN and the Carnegie Library of Pittsburgh, please refer to their web pages.

CASE STUDY 2

NorthStarNet and the Creation of Suburban Community

http://www.northstarnet.org/

According to the U.S. Census Bureau, about half of our nation's population now lives in the suburbs. The nature of the suburban landscape poses challenges for librarians working to build community in part simply because residents in suburbia are more dispersed than city dwellers. In addition, social institutions—be they community clubs or governmental offices—are more widely separated, and information about local concerns is harder to locate than it is in cities. As a result, a sense of community is more difficult to come by. That's not to say, in the words of Gertrude Stein, that "there is no there there" where the suburbs are concerned. On the contrary, suburbs can be varied, vibrant places with proud histories. Rather, it means that for suburbanites interested in finding information about their communities, getting "there" from here may require a greater effort. Suburban Chicago is a good case in point, as 1999–2000 ALA President and North Suburban Library System (NSLS) Director Sarah Long pointed out to us in a recent interview. Long characterized the difference between urban and suburban information seeking in this way:

> If you live in Chicago, you have the *Tribune,* you have the *Sun Times,* you have [local television stations], you have a city government, you have one city

library. Everything is focused on the entity itself. If you live in the suburbs, everything is fragmented. You probably live in one suburb, and work in another, and shop in a third. And you're not really mindful of boundaries as you pass them. You need information that's really hard to get.

NorthStarNet (NSN) community network, a partnership between NSLS and Suburban Library System (SLS), is designed to help bring Chicago's suburban communities together in virtual space even though they are dispersed in physical space. By linking together 124 communities, NorthStarNet makes life in Chicago's suburbs more cohesive.

NorthStarNet from the Inside Out

The administrative offices for NSLS provide funding, logistical and administrative support, servers, and technical assistance, as well as guidance on the long-term direction of NSN. The system is led by Long, who first envisioned an electronic CN for her system as a replacement for what she refers to as the "ratty little file," the difficult-to-maintain paper-based collections of CI resources that librarians gathered prior to computers coming to the fore. In the mid-1990s, Long worked with the State Library of Illinois to secure funding for what would become NSN. Although not involved in the day-to-day logistics of the network, her commitment to the power that CI can have in building communities is apparent in the work NSN does.

Melissa Henderson, the manager of NSN, oversees the day-to-day operation of the electronic CN. Although this position involves some technical know-how, Henderson sees it as "an outreach job, not a technology job." She works to bring more libraries into NSN. (Membership is not mandated by the system. This would undermine the decentralized nature of the network. More on that below.) In addition, Henderson helps member libraries add IPs, the NSN term for non-profit organizations, municipal agencies, and businesses that have sites hosted on the network. Her other responsibilities include developing curricula, policies, and procedures that improve NSN's effectiveness.

While the concept and the funding for NSN originated at North Suburban, SLS is also a primary partner in the network. Such cross-system collaboration is a rarity but has been a boon to NSN in a number of respects. For example, the State Library of Illinois looks favorably on partnerships between library systems. This might prove useful as NSN looks for future funding. In addition, having more libraries involved in NSN helps to ensure its long-term sustainability. One of Long's goals is to make NSN "indispensable" and SLS's involvement helps in that regard because the more communities become invested in the network, the more it can become a necessary tool in people's lives. Moreover, SLS's participation in NSN is a "value add" in many respects. As Sheree Kozel-La Ha, the administrative consultant for SLS NSN members, puts it: "Our participation has been good for NSN because I think it infused the network with energy. It encourages members to put a greater emphasis on marketing what NSN does, and it has brought more excitement to the system."

A Distributed Model

The evolutionary path NSN has taken since its inception is one in which form and function go hand in hand. Its service area spans six counties and 124 communities of varying sizes. There is no one center street that these communities are built around, no single governmental building that oversees the doings of the region's 1.6 million people. Rather, there are any number of main streets, shopping districts, libraries, and town halls. Therefore, it seems appropriate that the decentralized nature of the region be reflected in the organization of the regional information network. Unlike many of the urban networks that we have studied (for an example, please refer to case study 1, Pittsburgh's TRFN) where a more centralized community is served by a network originating from the city's main library, NSN's authority—like its constituency—is more spread out. Figure 3.4, which the NSN staff uses in community presentations, gives a sense for how the network is structured.

While this diagram depicts the NSN offices at North Suburban and SLS at the top of the network, the individual member libraries are placed squarely at its center. This is not mere window dressing on NSN's part. Rather, this is how the system really works. This library-centered vision was evident in the pitch that Long made to community libraries when the program began: "We'll take care of the hardware and the software, but you're the frontline people. Your library is the one that is empowered to go out into the community." This approach is still the rule today as Henderson notes: "North Suburban never wants to be the focus. It needs to be the library that is the focus in each community." To fulfill this role, each member library designates a person or two to serve as NSN library

FIGURE 3.4   NETWORK STRUCTURE FOR NORTHSTARNET

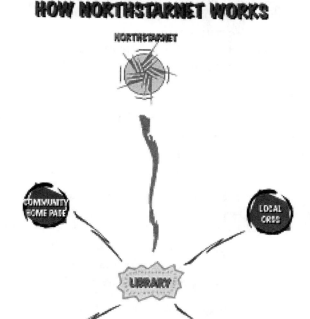

coordinator (LC). The LCs serve as liaisons between NSN and their individual communities. They work to recruit new IPs and to offer support to current providers. At present, there are nearly 1,000 IPs involved in NSN, ranging from local businesses to non-profit groups to government agencies. Each IP has a web page hosted on NSN that offers information on what the organization does, the services it offers, where it is located, key contact people, and so on.

Library representation in NSN decision-making is assured through the participation of two library-oriented advisory boards. The Operations Advisory Committee (OAC) consists of a group of eleven LCs as well as Henderson from NSLS and SLS's Kozel-La Ha and Jenny Levine. OAC was formed after the NSN grew too large (there are currently more than sixty member libraries) for decisions to all be made by group consensus.

Therefore NSN asked its more active, more vocal members to serve on the advisory committee. As Kathy Rolsing, the LC from the Park Ridge Public Library and member of the committee recalled, "Doing any kind of research or making decisions on something important was getting difficult in a group of over sixty coordinators. So we formed this advisory committee where we could discuss whatever was coming up among a smaller group."

While the OAC is composed of LCs who do the frontline work for the network, another group, the Policy and Planning Advisory Committee (PPAC), looks at larger issues facing NSN as a whole. PPAC is made up of directors from ten member libraries (along with administrators like Henderson and Kozel-La Ha from the library system offices). Henderson views the difference between PPAC and OAC in this way:

> The directors have a big picture view of the role NorthStarNet plays in their community and what a community information network is. Meanwhile, people in OAC tend to focus more closely on their library's part of [the] network. Perhaps it evolved that way because library coordinators are the hands-on people who actually get the phone calls from individual information providers who need help while the directors are more free to take a longer view.

OAC and PPAC both meet on a monthly basis. NSN also offers an electronic discussion list that participants can use to share ideas and field technical questions. In addition, NSN holds quarterly meetings of all LCs as well as semi-annual meetings of all participants including IPs. Henderson feels that, even with an electronic CN, such meetings in real time and space are important:

> These meetings are intended to give participants in NSN a larger sense of community and also, to emphasize how that can benefit them, being part of this larger community information network. I also want people to feel a little bit more ownership of the whole and responsibility to the whole—not just their site, but that their site is part of a larger project.

Many Roads to Community

While the various member libraries all share in NSN's mission of using the Internet to build community, the specifics of how they go about accomplishing this goal vary considerably from library to library. This level of autonomy is a hallmark of NSN. And it pays off because this freedom means that each individual library has greater flexibility to reflect its community online. One result of library autonomy is that NSN comes across not as one large site but rather as a gateway to a collection of smaller community sites that are referred to as Communities on the Web. Under the NSN umbrella you'll find links to sites like La Grange Community, NorthStarNet Arlington Heights, the Park Ridge Community Network, and SkokieNet. All of these sites are housed on the NSN server and coordinated by LCs at member libraries, and yet they all have their own domain names, their own look and feel, and, to a certain extent, their own policies and procedures.

Such an approach can occasionally be something of a double-edged sword. Because member libraries have a great amount of latitude to determine the form that their Community on the Web will take, some inconsistency across the system is inevitable. For example, some member libraries are very much invested in NSN and have LCs on staff for whom the network is a primary responsibility. In those instances, the NSN community sites tend to be quite well developed, with more extensive and up-to-date content and more vital relationships with community groups that serve as IPs. At the other end of the spectrum are less active libraries. In these cases, the library's LC has less time, and perhaps less interest, to spend on NSN. These are LCs who, in Henderson's words, "have NorthStarNet as one of twelve things they do in their library." Likewise, because libraries usually set their own policies regarding look and feel, content, and so on, the network is less cohesive than it might otherwise be. In fact, on many of the network's sites, there is no visual element or text that suggests that the page being viewed is part of NSN. As a result, the casual user might not realize what a powerful, comprehensive tool is available, and IPs don't necessarily get the added credibility that comes from being a part of a larger network.

Henderson views the plusses and minuses of a distributed information network philosophically: "There are so many things in life where you have great benefits from a certain type of system, but also an equal number of challenges. Our system isn't the easiest way to do things. It's not. But it probably is the best way." After all, without a great deal of autonomy, member libraries would not have the flexibility to create sites that best reflect their individual communities—a capability that Henderson views as NSN's greatest strength: "The biggest advantage NorthStarNet has is the fact that the libraries are very attuned to what goes on in their community and they want to be."

The Park Ridge Community Network (see figure 3.5) and SkokieNet (see figure 3.6) are two examples that show the different forms that library membership in NSN can take:

Park Ridge Community Network

Kathy Rolsing, the LC for the Park Ridge Public Library, strives to guarantee that her community's NSN site, the Park Ridge Community Network, be embraced not only by the library but also by the larger community as well: "We didn't want people to say, 'Oh, that's that library project that they're working on over there.' Instead, we wanted them to say, 'That's the Park Ridge Community project.'" To build community buy-in, Rolsing has gathered together important players from the Park Ridge area—including representatives from the school system, the park district, city hall, and the chamber of commerce—to serve as an advisory committee for the network. Rolsing describes the character of the advisory committee in this way: "It's a place where we can ask important questions about the role of the Park Ridge Community Network. What do we want for our community? What are your ideas? How can we improve our sites? How can we attract more information providers?" Our research team had a chance to sit in on an advisory committee meeting during our visit and

FIGURE 3.5   SAMPLE SCREEN OF LOGO FROM PARK RIDGE
                     COMMUNITY NETWORK

we saw just how important committee meetings could be in the generation and sharing of ideas. Oftentimes, one committee member would mention a procedure that worked for her, followed by the sound of scratching pens as others made notes to themselves to try it.

Rolsing also notes that the committee stands by her when decisions have to be made that affect Park Ridge's 110 IPs: "I always know that if I ever have a problem with enforcement of policy or creation of policy, the community will back me up. I've always got the advisory committee behind me so that people can't say, 'That was Kathy's stupid decision. I don't agree with it.' I always have them there." Not only do committee members diffuse potential problems, they also serve as ambassadors to the community, increasing the public's awareness of the network.

One challenge that Park Ridge, like all of NSN's member libraries, faces is finding ways to make it easier for community groups and businesses—many of which are not particularly Internet savvy—to create web pages that explain their organizations' missions and activities. Rolsing offers her IPs a particularly innovative solution to this problem. She links organizations that want websites with budding web designers from the computer club at the local high school. For a very reasonable fee, these students will create websites for IPs.

With SkokieNet, the Skokie Public Library takes a different approach to providing online CI than does Park Ridge (or, indeed, most of the other NSN member libraries). Rather than focusing on encouraging neighborhood organizations and businesses to build their own web pages, Skokie-Net maintains an online directory of organizations. Frances Roehm, the

FIGURE 3.6   SAMPLE SCREEN OF LOGO FROM SKOKIENET

Welcome to

SKOKIENET

Building Community on the Web

LC for SkokieNet, describes how it works: "We have volunteers who assist us in gathering information from local organizations. And we enter it—also with the help of volunteers—into an Access database. After that, using a template, we create basic web pages for these groups." As a result of these efforts, SkokieNet now boasts 500 organization directory listings. Most listings feature contact information for the organization in question as well as hours of operation, a brief description of what the group does, and in many cases, an email link. Maintenance of the database is fairly labor intensive for the library. However, this approach came out of a realization about the community organizations that SkokieNet serves. As Roehm notes,

> Many of our information providers are small clubs, businesses, or non-profit organizations that have no one on hand to do Web work. And the groups feel overloaded with their other responsibilities anyway. Therefore, it's a big help to them to get even basic information out there through SkokieNet's directory listings.

Roehm goes on to say that disseminating information is not an end in itself: "What makes SkokieNet listings truly valuable is the fact that visibility for the organization also means getting the info to someone who can use it. It's a win-win situation."

Perhaps Roehm's appreciation for the challenges that IPs face comes in part from the fact that she is not simply an LC, she is also an IP. Roehm oversees ChicagoJobs.org, a very extensive resource for locating employment in the Chicagoland area that is hosted by NSN.

NSN Means Business

NSN hosts pages for local businesses as well as those for non-profits and government agencies. As with many things on the network, member libraries choose whether or not to invite businesses to join their Community on the Web. While some member libraries feel that free server space should only be made available for the non-profit community, others embrace a business presence on their sites. As Rolsing puts it, "As far as we're concerned, businesses are part of the community. They pay taxes. Our philosophy was, how could I not have the chamber of commerce involved? How could we eliminate the business community and expect this to be a viable method?" In addition, Henderson notes that many of the suburban communities that NSN serves do not have a central location with "a boys' club or a garden club. But, oftentimes, there are a lot of businesses in these areas." Therefore, in these communities businesses are a natural constituency for NSN.

Indicators of Impact:
"Too Good to Be True?"

To get a better sense for the type of impact that working with NSN has on local organizations, we conducted several IP focus groups. One participant had a particularly memorable comment: "NSN sounds too good to be true, but it is true." And, certainly, the free server space, technology training, and exposure that many organizations garner through their association with NSN seem almost unbelievable at times. And yet the benefits, both for IPs and the libraries they work with, are quite real. Here are a few of the many success stories we uncovered over the course of our research:

According to an officer at a municipal police department, his relationship with his NSN library has made a major difference in the department's community policing efforts. Working with his library coordinator, he has developed a series of workshops on Internet crime and safety.

A local chapter of a choral group notes that their NSN website has served as an effective recruitment tool for new singers.

A staff person from a local historical society indicates that her group receives frequent requests for information via email: "I can't believe all the wonderful people we've met through the Internet. The other day, we received a note from someone who said, 'Thank so much for all your help in my search. I've been looking for this information for years. You've given me new avenues to explore.'"

A representative from an area parenting organization told us how her group took a member's extensive list of area activities for families and made it available on their NSN website. By making information that would otherwise be hard to get readily available, the group is better able to serve its clientele.

Many organizations use their NSN-hosted web pages to give the public a better sense for the work that they do. For example, a member of a local chapter of the Lions Club feels that his organization can make itself more "relevant to the world" by advertising their public service activities (e.g., the free eyeglasses and eye exams they provide for the needy) online. Similarly, a member of an area chapter of the Veterans of Foreign Wars (VFW) believes that the group's website can be used to change public perceptions of the VFW: "We want to promote ourselves and defy the stereotype of a bunch of old guys sitting around. We do quite a bit of community service. A number of us volunteer at the local school."

A Different View of the Library

As we have seen, it is certainly the case that local organizations can alter public perceptions of their groups through their association with a library-based CN. Interestingly enough, the reverse is also true: A library can transform its public image by working with local groups to create a CN. Long told us a story that makes this point nicely. One day a library director came to her, overjoyed by the way in which the local business community had warmed to her library due to its participation in NSN. She told Long, "Finally the chamber man is coming to me." The library had proven itself to the chamber of commerce through its community building and Internet savvy. Steve Moskal, the director of the La Grange Public Library, shared a similar story:

> One day, I was sitting in a La Grange Business Association meeting minding my own business, and someone asked, "When are we going to get our website?" His friend responded by saying, "That guy over there in the pink shirt, Steve, he's going to build our website for us." That's when I knew that I'd suddenly been catapulted into being this technology wizard.

What is it about NSN that has brought about this elevation in the status of librarianship? Kozel-La Ha of SLS has a theory:

> I remember being part of a small library and wanting the respect of the whole community. And yet, I knew that this wasn't really a possibility because for so many people, I had nothing to offer. But now, being at the center of NSN, we get that respect. And in some cases, respect can translate into very concrete public support. For example, the Ela Area public library recently passed a referendum by a scant 94 votes. The library's director is convinced that the measure wouldn't have passed if the library hadn't developed a strong relationship with community agencies and organizations through its work on NSN.

CASE STUDY 3

CascadeLink: A Vehicle for Fostering Community Connections

http://www.cascadelink.org/

Portland, Oregon, is a rare example of a city that continually challenges the conventional wisdom that urban growth is unequivocally good. Especially at a time when most American cities have expanded with little regard for the hazards of urban sprawl, Portland has been one city that recognizes the virtues of limited growth. As a result, while other American cities have become plagued with the problems caused by urban sprawl, such as smog, poor public transportation, and impoverished urban centers, Portland, in contrast, is looked to as a model in urban planning and development. James Howard Kunstler, author of the book *The Geography of Nowhere,* attributes Portland's success to its unique emphasis on the connections and cooperation built between organizations, city institutions, and the city's inhabitants. Kunstler writes:

> Oregonians are acting intelligently and setting an example in regional land-use policy that the rest of the nation would do well to heed. In Portland they have a city of which they deserve to feel proud . . . [civic-minded Portlanders] understand that the city is only as good as its connections, and that urban ingredients treated in isolation have no meaning (James Howard Kunstler, *Geography of Nowhere,* 1993, 206).

For decades, Portland's public servants have been keenly aware of the need for networking and coalition building among the city's institutions and organizations. Without cooperation from business people, government officials, and non-profits, the city would not have been as successful implementing its unprecedented urban policy. One noteworthy innovation is the city's urban-growth boundary, a land-use plan that strictly marks the boundaries between urban and rural areas in order to promote the efficient use of urban land, public facilities, and services while preserving prime farm and forest lands outside the boundary. That plus an emphasis on public transportation over automobiles has resulted in a city with a vibrant downtown and dynamic neighborhoods free of the smog and gridlock that plague other urban centers. Portland is a city of proud, distinct neighborhoods that work together to produce a vigorous city where quality of life is highly regarded.

On our case-study visit to Portland, we discovered that this integrated approach is business as usual for the community's library. The Multnomah County Library (http://www.multcolib.org/) operates in the same capacity by building relationships with the other government agencies, organizations, and civic institutions. In fact, while the library stands at the physical center of the city, CascadeLink (http://www.cascadelink.org/), the library-supported CN, might well be considered its virtual center (see figure 3.7).

CascadeLink is a regional CN that serves Clackamas, Multnomah, and Washington counties in Oregon and Clark County in Washington (Portland's neighbor across the Columbia River). It offers CI organized by subject, covering such topics as neighborhoods, jobs, arts and entertainment, and elections, among others. CascadeLink also features the most widely used and standardized community calendar for the region. In addition, the site links directly to the library's community organization database (COOL), which provides listings of more than 5,500 organizations from throughout Oregon and southwest Washington. This impressive collection of resources would not be possible were it not for the position that the library has in the Portland community.

The Library's Instrumental Role

The Multnomah County Library (MCPL) serves as a point of convergence for government agencies, non-profit organizations, and educational institutions in the city. CascadeLink evolved in 1995 out of meetings among representatives from such important regional institutions as Metro

FIGURE 3.7   SAMPLE SCREEN FROM CASCADELINK

Regional government, MCPL (see figure 3.8) and other area libraries, Portland State University, Multnomah County, the City of Portland, Oregon Civic Network Coalition, Portland Office of Neighborhood Associations, Portland Public Schools, Tualatin Valley Community Access, U.S. Representative Furse's office, and U.S. West Communications. But it was MCPL that spearheaded the charge by hiring a CI System Program Specialist and launching the project.

It is the partnership between all these groups that gives CascadeLink its strength. Donna Reed, the director of Cascade-Link, describes the relationship among CascadeLink's various actors in the following way: "The county really supports Cascade-Link with all the other partners playing into CascadeLink, and there is a relationship because our role is to organize the information and to advocate it." Thus the library builds upon its unique role as information organizer, a trusted neutral agency, and community advocate to uphold a project that is well appreciated by its constituents. Ginnie Cooper, MCPL library director, told us she strongly believes in the community value of this project: "It is important to make sure that that information is available to the community. And when I say that information, I mean from a variety of different sources, the library's only one of them. That's more important than that people know that this is a library program." Still, as a result of the library's leading role in CascadeLink, the library has earned greater credibility along with the necessary buy-in required to make a project like CascadeLink successful.

FIGURE 3.8 SAMPLE SCREEN FROM MULTNOMAH COUNTY LIBRARY

Partnerships Are Central to the Project

How do these partnerships work? For starters, once a month, a Cascade-Link steering committee convenes to discuss the future direction of the website. The group is comprised of important community players, such as government agency staff, civil servants, and representatives from the school system and regional organizations. According to CascadeLink's Reed, involvement by such a wide variety of stakeholders is critical. In addition to sharing its vision for the future of CascadeLink, the steering committee works hard to promote and build upon the site. This is accomplished in a variety of ways. For example, committee members raise CascadeLink's profile by linking to the site from their organizations' pages. In addition, the group organizes such events as an annual technology summit as a way to invite additional organizations and agencies to the table. Aside from being a great way to promote the value of this one-stop regional resource, the summit also provides technology training and planning for area organizations and businesses.

Bringing so many stakeholders into the same room each month has resulted in other benefits for the CascadeLink site and the community at large. A recently launched website designed to help Portland area businesses (http://www.BusinessInPortland.org/) is a powerful example of this partnership in action. The city developed this Web portal to provide small-business owners with advice on networking in the business community, as well as training and assistance information and examples of business best practices, among other resources. As a result of participating on the CascadeLink board, the Portland city staff recognize that the business portal's audience is CascadeLink's audience, and vice versa. The staff members say that they better understand how to represent and organize information for their audience thanks to lessons they've learned from CascadeLink. Today, CascadeLink prominently links to the new city business portal. CascadeLink, in turn, fulfills its goals of providing the community with current information created by the experts.

The CascadeLink staff has also played an important role in developing partnerships between the county (http://www.co.multnomah.or.us/maps/) and Portland State University (http://www.upa.pdx.edu/IMS/psuhome/psuhome.html/) as they explore ways in which to make Geographic Information Systems (GIS) data more accessible to the public. Ultimately, CascadeLink staff are working toward making it possible for Web users to be able to download demographic and environmental-based maps from their computers (see figure 3.9). This could enable community

FIGURE 3.9   SAMPLE SCREEN OF LOGO FROM MULTNOMAH COUNTY GIS

groups and citizens to demonstrate problem areas in their communities while advocating for policy improvements. Furthermore, CascadeLink has facilitated relationship building with community GIS experts in an effort to share resources for citizen and community benefits.

The staff at CascadeLink deserves credit for the proactive way in which it has facilitated relationships within their community. After all, partnerships are rarely forged overnight. The CascadeLink staff's persistence and the library's perceived neutrality helps to build trust among the community players and CascadeLink. As Reed put it: "I try to get myself invited to meetings all the time, particularly with people who do things regionally that marry up with what CascadeLink is all about. I try to go to the community or governmental communicators meetings and to the regional health informational sharing meeting." This sort of persistence has yielded impressive results, many of which benefit CascadeLink's largest group of stakeholders—the citizens of Portland.

Citizens as Stakeholders: Promoting Community Involvement

CascadeLink's mission states that it "provides online community information, encourages citizen involvement, and supports Internet access for people living in the Portland, OR, and Vancouver, WA, region." CascadeLink's message regarding citizen participation rings loud and clear by encouraging public submissions to the site. In a sense, "ordinary" citizens are just as much partners in CascadeLink as the government and nonprofit organizations because CascadeLink asks for feedback and submissions throughout the site. It is hard to miss one of their "Send comments, questions, and suggestions" links located on every page of the site. In addition, CascadeLink provides special online forms by which users can contribute to the community calendar (http://calendar.cascadelink.org/). The CN also offers online forms for users to submit additional organizations, access points, educational opportunities, or links to the county listings. The CascadeLink staff feels strongly that the site is what it is today because they regularly receive feedback and suggestions from their audience.

Of course, the site would not be as extensive as it is if it relied on public submissions alone. CascadeLink has a crew of volunteers and staff who maintain the various areas of the site. For example, a librarian from TRI-Met, the regional transportation department, maintains the transportation pages (http://www.cascadelink.org/trans/index.html/), thus covering an area of great importance to many Portlanders. There is also a librarian at a fishes and wildlife agency who enriches the environmental (http://www.cascadelink.org/env/index.html/) section of CascadeLink. Furthermore, the CascadeLink staff reaches out to the community in a number of ways familiar to all CI librarians such as talking to residents on the buses, reading relevant newspaper articles, attending community meetings, and making contact with representatives from all parts of the community.

The CascadeLink staff is proud of the fact that the CN reflects the diversity of the community. This is in keeping with the mission of the library. "That's one of those things that I say all the time—that the library is information neutral. It can represent the entire community," says Reed. In fact, staff culls information for the events calendar from all over the city by monitoring a wide range of resources, including neighborhood newsletters, hospital pamphlets, specialty magazines, business flyers, and organizational brochures. Thus health-fair events are listed next to religious ceremonies and salsa classes. The diversity of events represented on the events calendar (http://calendar.cascadelink.org/) is so extensive and diverse that *The Oregonian,* the local newspaper, points to CascadeLink's calendar from their website.

Specializing in Community Information

CascadeLink offers a great deal more than just information regarding upcoming events or results of regional elections. Visitors to CascadeLink told us that they use the site for a variety of reasons. They use it to find jobs, access neighborhood profiles, identify educational resources, locate non-profit organizations, gather demographic data, and track down information on ordinances and zoning laws. Librarians are skilled information organizers. So, it comes as little surprise that the CI on CascadeLink is easy to navigate, well-organized, and frequently updated. The benefit of accessing CI from a site like CascadeLink is perhaps best described by the users. They sing its praises with comments such as the following:

> This site contains a wealth of information specific to the Portland metro area and is one of my favorites.

> It brings everything to one location. It's very easy to navigate around in and everything is right there at your fingertips—it's just right there.

> I absolutely rely on this website for home and work projects. I also refer lots of people I speak [with] from both out of state and locally, to the website. It cuts through all the garbage and gets straight to the heart!

Pounding the Pavement on the Information Highway

According to a survey that we conducted with CascadeLink users, hunting for employment is by far the most popular use of the CascadeLink site. The majority of people who responded to our online survey said that they came to CascadeLink to check out the job and career pages (http://www.cascadelink.org/jobs/index.html/). One job seeker said, "CascadeLink is really the best place to go to find out about jobs—all the information is right there. You can find out about benefits, the salary—all on the website." Meanwhile, another job seeker described the arduous path that he would have had to take were it not for electronic information resources such as CascadeLink: "I would have to go directly to the locations to apply for the job, but that would take a lot of time. It is much easier to use CascadeLink. It's a great time saver." These quotes are telling of the ways in which CascadeLink staff embrace today's technological innovations in order to respond to citizens' information needs.

Outcomes of Vision— Pavements to Parks

Portland is a unique city that tends to defy the same forces that have negatively affected other American cities. James Howard Kunstler describes the story of how back in the 1970s, at a time when other American cities eagerly accepted federal subsidies to build new freeways along their water-fronts, Portland opted to tear down a four-lane expressway along the river. They replaced the expressway with two miles of a riverfront park in an effort to reconnect the city with its waterfront. This story illuminates the forward thinking of the city's inhabitants and planners, while it pro-vides an anecdote about the power of partnership. When residents and their governing institutions work together to define what's important, they can come up with thoughtful and satisfying solutions. There is no doubt that the same forward-thinking vision exhibited by Portland's planners is also reflected in their CN, CascadeLink. Indeed, the success of CascadeLink reflects the power of partnership and the expertise of librar-ians to organize information and advocate for their community.

Community Networks
as Information Communities

Information Communities—a New Term
with Potential to Develop a Larger Framework

CNs are not a household word among librarians. The 14% participation rate in CNs suggests that 86% of public libraries are not engaged in this activity. Projects that are outside of the mainstream are vulnerable to administration changes and budget cuts. More than one long-term CI librarian shared information with us anecdotally that indicated reversals of library involvement in intensive community networking activities due to lack of understanding of the approach and value of what appeared to be an isolated activity. CNs need to be viewed within a larger framework. We suggest that librarians consider this phenomenon as an example of an "information community," a term that cuts across types of library lines and moves the emphasis first to the need for information and thus away from the collections as the first consideration.

The term information community is even newer than CNs. Like CNs, this term is neither widely used nor understood. Yet it has the potential to develop a framework that cuts across types of library and institutional boundaries.

An information community (IC) is "a constituency united by a common interest in a set of dynamic, linked, and varying resources."[1] An IC is "[a] partnership of institutions and individuals forming and cultivating a community of interest around the provision and exchange of information, or knowledge, aimed at increasing access to that information or increasing communication, and thereby increasing that knowledge."[2] The American Library Association's Library Administration and Management Association defined the term and has taken steps to foster its adoption. By this definition, CNs are excellent examples of ICs.

To understand the concept of ICs we describe below several partnerships that can be called ICs. The Information Communities website at the University of Michigan (http://www.si.umich.edu/helpseek/Resources/index.html#InfoCommunities/) provides examples of ICs, including those that have arisen completely outside of libraries and function (to their detriment) without the guidance of librarians.

Attributes of Information Communities

While, like each CN, each IC is unique, common patterns may be seen. They may cut across type of library lines, involve collaboration with a variety of organizations as well as some sort of resource sharing (including in-kind contributions) to become the responsibility of more than one organization. Given the state of information technology, they, like CNs, are likely to be dynamic and distributed. Since ICs form around people's need to get and use information, they may have a fairly well-developed constituent group, and their leaders may have an understanding of how the constituency uses information. The circumstances surrounding each IC may differ; however most ICs owe their creation and development to the values of librarians. The desire to increase access and the interest in better understanding the need for and use of information as well as the knowledge, abilities, and approaches of librarians in knowing the community and in understanding how to organize information and collaborate and share resources effectively are basic skills librarians possess.

ICs exploit the information-sharing qualities of the Internet. As a result, they incorporate diverse IPs, use collaborative approaches, make effective use of information technologies, communicate across geographic and other barriers, and adopt entrepreneurial approaches. CNs form in a geographic area because community leaders realize that resources are often scattered throughout the community and thus are less accessible to the people who need them. Other ICs develop because of the common need to create, disseminate, and use information more effectively throughout a community of interest.

Like CN leaders, other librarians have learned that the Internet is the perfect medium to create new and enhanced access to knowledge and information, particularly distributed resources. In addition, as leaders of ICs, librarians make effective use of bringing people, especially IPs, together. They may also provide training or mentoring opportunities to assure that the clientele make effective use of the information.

Other Examples of Information Communities

THE MAKING OF ANN ARBOR

ICs can be constructed to bring together digital resources for the benefit of a geographic community. "The Making of Ann Arbor" (MOAA) (http: //www.aadl.org/moaa/index2.htm/) is one such example. MOAA represents an attempt to develop an IC within a single geographic region that transcends the boundaries traditionally separating libraries. MOAA is an illustrated narrative about Ann Arbor from its pioneer days when it was part of the Michigan Territory to the early twentieth century. The project draws upon the expertise and resources of the Ann Arbor District Library, the University of Michigan's Bentley Historical Society and the University of Michigan Digital Library Initiative to build a website utilized by those with an interest in historic Ann Arbor. In addition to the illustrated narrative history of the city the website has a searchable image database, including many photographs and other visual images not used in the narrative.

The MOAA partners view their initial collaborative efforts as the foundation for an ongoing, evolving project about the history of Ann Arbor and have stated:

> In envisioning future plans, we plan to add more narrative to bring the city's history forward in time, to contribute additional historical materials in digital form, and to extend our partnership by seeking other collaborators in the community who will enrich the site with historical narratives, photographs, and other materials about Ann Arbor, its people, businesses, and organizations.[3]

Three elements were required to take on this digital project: historical content, technical skills in the digital arena, and experience and expertise in working with a wide and diverse public.

> Over the years, the three partner institutions collectively have accumulated a rich documentary and visual history of Ann Arbor and surrounding areas; the institutions have developed a strong staff expert in working in the digital

arena; and they have each interacted with students at all levels, local history enthusiasts, and other citizens interested in the forces and events that have defined Ann Arbor. Each partner has made invaluable contributions to The Making of Ann Arbor.[4]

The success of this type of IC depends not only on cutting across library lines and communicating with schools, teachers, local newspapers, non-profit groups, and genealogists who need and use these resources but also on taking advantage of the strengths of each institution while adding greater value to the community. The result is that these three institutions have brought the early history of Ann Arbor to life by creating a Web-accessible, digital collection of information and images.

LA AS SUBJECT

Another fine example of an IC with a geographic basis is "LA as Subject" (http://www.getty.edu/gri/public/lasubject.htm/). LA as Subject was a four-year research project designed to facilitate the critical recovery of historical narratives about Los Angeles. Its goal was to illuminate diverse and unique archives and collections and examine their role in the transmission of cultural values through lectures, symposia, exhibitions, and public forums.[5] LA as Subject represents an IC developed as a result of a partnership between the Getty Research Institute and twenty-five "lending institutions" in the Los Angeles area including local private collections as well as universities. The archives, collections, monuments, and cultural practices included in this exhibit are the vehicles used to bring together diverse communities and individuals of the past into the present.

HEALTHWEB

HealthWeb is a collaborative project of more than twenty health sciences libraries supported by the National Library of Medicine (NLM) (see http://healthweb.org/members.cfm/ for the entire list of participating libraries). In 1994 a group of health-sciences librarians from institutions affiliated with the Committee for Institutional Cooperation (CIC) decided that their work with health-sciences professionals, as well as their knowledge of, access to, and ability to use these resources, would be greatly enhanced if they worked together. Their constituency—healthcare professionals—is demanding, and the information it needs has life and death implications. This project began as the expansion of the Internet and the Web was just beginning, and they decided to work cooperatively to "develop an interface which will provide organized access to evaluated non-commercial, health-related, Internet-accessible resources."[6] The resources for HealthWeb include those currently available as well as new resources developed in collaboration with other organizations. The developers of HealthWeb visualized an interface designed "to integrate educational information so the user has a one-stop entry point to learn skills and use material relevant to their discipline."[7]

In sum, the use of the term "information communities" is still in its infancy. Yet it seems to be a useful vehicle to show that CNs not only share approaches with a number of other initiatives that are need-centered and focused on the use of information rather than its collection, it also shows that CNs are in a leadership position. That term encompasses all types of libraries and can be used to identify the exciting emerging models and the benefits that they bring both to the communities and to the institutions they serve. ICs may help librarians see the connections among a variety of externally focused initiatives (and thus make them less likely to be considered orphans in library service). Adoption of a common term will also help professionals learn to share their vision and recognize commonality of situations, circumstances, approaches, strategies, and benefits that will result from the creation of ICs.

Information Communities

Using a variety of approaches and data sources, this chapter has identified a number of ways that public libraries across the nation participate in CNs, excellent examples of what has recently become known as "information communities." This chapter has shown that librarians involved in CNs see participation as an extension of what they have done for at least thirty years. Since CNs are local phenomena, the CN reflects its community and the leadership styles and approaches of the public library.

We have found that all CNs in our study have taken a leadership role in helping the community understand itself by increasing access to the community's information. All use the power of the Web to virtually depict the community. They increase access to information by and about local non-profits and other organizations, health and social-services agencies, libraries, museums and educational institutions, businesses and employers, and local and state governments.

These CNs bring together information created by a number of organizations including, but not limited to, the library and add value to CI by providing one-stop shopping for CI. The best practice CNs we examined help the community keep track of its events by creating, hosting, or linking to a community calendar. Some CNs invest in information infrastructure for the good of the community—a server, software, tech support, etc.—and in the process allow non-profits to put their scarce resources to work directly for their clientele. CNs add value by modeling collaboration among organizations and providing training to community leaders in technology use and developing a Web presence. As a result, CNs function as catalysts for educational, social, and economic growth and bring a wide range of benefits to the community.

We have shown that a CN reflects the mission of its parent organization, and, just as importantly, the knowledge, skills, and values of librarians. Library CN leaders are able to assess situations and local conditions and each CN model seeks to solve a local access problem or improve existing access. The actual CN model will build on the examination and consideration of a variety of community and library circumstances. The models themselves consist of a range of content development and service considerations. Often staff recognize the need to provide training and technical assistance to community organizations and non-profit groups. Librarian CN partners are likely to convene or otherwise bring community organizations together (through Web technology, electronic discussion lists, etc.). They show community groups the value of linking to related organizations. CN leaders foster communication among community organizations, finding that it leads to the creation of new partnerships among community groups. The CN is a mechanism for modeling activities that result in increased collaboration, volunteerism, training, and other community-building activities. The next chapter presents the types of benefits that accrue from participation in CNs.

REFERENCES

1. This definition was prepared in conjunction with the LAMA Institute of the Year Committee. See http://www.si.umich.edu/helpseek/InfoCommunities/index.html/.

2. http://www.si.umich.edu/helpseek/InfoCommunities/workshop.html/.

3. http://www.aadl.org/moaa/index2.htm/.

4. Ibid.

5. http://www.si.umich.edu/helpseek/InfoCommunities/examples.html/.

6. http://healthweb.org/aboutus.cfm/.

7. Ibid.

4

Benefits of Access to Community Information and Community Networks

This chapter answers the following questions: "How does posting information on the Internet help?" and "How do service providers perceive posting information on the Internet will help clients and their organizations?" Since we framed our study from the perspective of the user, we were able to obtain numerous instances of how CI helps from a variety of context-centered perspectives. The findings in this chapter were drawn both from the national survey of CI librarians and the people interviewed in the course of our CN case studies. The discussion of these research questions shows many of the ways that CI librarians and those who are building CNs contribute to the social fabric of their communities.

Benefits of Networked Community Information

Although we found that librarians believe that their current evaluation tools are grossly inadequate to evaluate the public's use of CI, many, when asked, were able to identify ways that the community used CI. Fifty-four percent said that they remembered a time recently when they had learned how someone or some group had made use of CI. We received scores of examples from librarians responding to our survey. This kind of data, however, is haphazardly collected, if at all.

Following are examples of benefits submitted by CI librarians. The responses represent only a few of the answers to our question,

Can you remember a time recently when you learned how someone or some group made use of or benefited from CI? If yes, please provide us with one or two examples of how a *person* (adult or child), *government agency, non-profit organization, community,* or *citizen group* used or benefited from CI.

These benefits, filtered through librarians, resulted both from use of information in the library's CI database and from personal assistance from a librarian. To indicate the cumulative impact of anecdotal data, we have grouped responses into several representative categories of impact. These reflect the patterns in the data submitted—personal assistance or empowerment, value resulting from connecting people with other people and groups, neighborhood improvement, and community building. Thus, the section below reflects a few of the ways that CI made an impact on the lives of people in the community. Others include skill and confidence building, employment and educational gains, and increased knowledge of the community. Many of these are potential indicators of increased social capital.

People Report Personal, Neighborhood, and Community Benefits

Personal Assistance or Empowerment

Every year about five adults collect information on how to get their GED, register for the test, and pass with assistance provided at the library. Help ranges from providing basic directional information to help taking a practice test to one-on-one tutorial assistance.

A single mother with three children called. Her boyfriend (father of two of the kids) had left, taken their money, and is nowhere to be found. We referred her to local agencies to get help with emergency food, diapers, personal-care items, school shoes and clothing for the oldest child, and where to get copies of the children's birth certificates that the boyfriend took with him.

A person who was setting up a small business needed advice on licensing requirements. She used our community directory for lists of organizations to contact, our website, the electronic small-business directory produced by us, and our print resources. She later sent us a very complimentary email.

Value Resulting from Connecting People with Other People and Groups

Throughout our study people made a distinction between getting information about the community and information that would help them make connections with other people and organizations. Librarians at present do not make these kinds of distinctions, and this lack of awareness may limit the ability of some people to obtain the information they need to make connections.

> A concerned relative from halfway across the country was able to contact one of our senior-citizen services to check on her elderly relative.

> Librarians [on our staff] report connecting patrons to support groups and counseling services, assisting grandparents seeking custody of grandchildren, adults looking to adopt, and PTAs looking for speakers.

> The library has patrons looking for specific types of groups. For example, one man wanted to join a male chorus like the one he was in where he had previously lived. The library provided him with a name, and he is now a member of that group.

> An individual wanted to home-school her children. She used the CI database to locate other home-schooling parents and joined a related organization.

> There was a tragic fire in our city last Christmas that claimed the lives of a father and all but one of his children. The fire department asked the library to suggest some social-service organizations and community groups that could offer aid to the surviving mother and child. The library created a potential referral list using the CI database.

> An organization that administers our hospital told us that many of their patients use the CI database to locate support services for themselves in preparation for leaving the hospital. A brochure is placed on each meal tray to promote use of the service.

Contributions to Neighborhood Improvement

A couple has just bought a home that has a pond declared "wetlands" by the state. Using the new GIS (geographic and aerial photo database) the couple has the evidence needed to get department of transportation and department of environmental management to help clear the pond of sand and salt from winter road work that caused a large sandbar in the pond, reducing aquatic life substantially.

The library has a number of old pictures of residences. These have been helpful to people trying to restore older homes.

With the help of the library's photo collection, volunteers based the construction of a children's playground on a building in one of the historic photographs.

Community Building

A ministry group at a community church used the library's CI database as part of their sixteen-week training program. Volunteers learned about specific agencies here in the county that can help their parishioners when dealing with problems, such as a crisis intervention organization, a mental health association, and family services group.

The library-hosted local government website prompted a neighbor to exclaim how helpful it was to find city information on the Web readily available outside of the city's office hours.

A local agency wanted to issue a grant for improved education for unwed mothers. The agency used the library's CI database to determine the recipient of this $100,000 grant.

In spite of the fact that more than half of the CI staff were able to identify a use made of CI, most said that they do not have the tools they need to capture and use the kind of information identified above that could, with some effort, be used in evaluating what difference public library CI services make.

Benefits of a Community Network

The CNs we visited in Pittsburgh, the Chicago area, and Portland serve as powerful examples of what can happen when a community pools its resources to better inform the public. Our site visits to the three communities provided us with rich data obtained from interviews, focus groups, and examination of resource materials. Our respondents represented social-services agencies, non-profit organizations, and local government units. (Throughout this book, these organizations are called interchangeably, "service providers," "non-profit organizations and local government agencies," and "information providers.") We also interviewed the librarians who created, developed, and nurtured these CNs as well as the administrators of their library systems. Finally, we surveyed and interviewed users of CNs who were engaged in seeking information from the CN. We found that those involved with their local CN were able to identify in their own words a range of benefits that accrue to themselves and to the community.

The examples in this section demonstrate some of the many ways in which a local CN benefits community organizations, their constituents, and ultimately the larger community. Key questions are: What do service providers themselves see as the value of the CN? How do these community organizations that librarians call information providers, or IPs, perceive that posting information on the Internet helps their organizations and their clientele? The following section answers that question using the words of those we interviewed.

As we organized their responses we found that IPs had identified a number of ways that the CN benefited them. We found that a CN can:

Overcome barriers, including geographical and digital divide barriers and the reluctance to ask for information

Increase the effectiveness of non-profit organizations and help them become more responsive to the community

Increase people's ability to access relevant information

Help non-profits and government agencies become IPs and value librarians' knowledge and values

Contribute to community building, foster civic engagement, and create a sense of community

The benefits identified by these groups are powerful indicators that public libraries make strong contributions to the vitality of their communities. The challenge to evaluators is to translate these into indicators of impact.

A CN Can Help Overcome Geographical Barriers, Digital Divide Barriers, and Personal Reluctance to Ask for Information

The need of IPs and citizens in our study to connect to people confirms the research that goes back to Dervin's seminal work in the 1970s (1976). Increasing connections among organizations and individuals requires overcoming barriers. Barriers identified by our respondents included a community's geography (discussed in detail in each of the case-study profiles), the digital divide (seen here to encompass the barriers faced by those in poverty as well as the disabled), or barriers associated with people's inability or reluctance to ask for information (most often about sensitive topics). CNs bridge the digital divide in various ways; they can build capacity among non-profit organizations that serve low-income families, at-risk groups, and people with disabilities. CNs can provide content relevant to citizens (found to be a barrier by a national study of low-income groups and the Internet), which can also serve to bridge the digital divide.

Geographical Barriers Reduced

CNs in our study harnessed the power of the Internet to bring together previously unconnected individuals and groups by diminishing the barriers of physical distance. We illustrate this in the profiles of all three CNs.

As the staff from a group that offers support services to low-income single parents told their CN, "People across the country and even the world are learning about our organization—people that we could not reach otherwise."

An arts agency in Pennsylvania used its website to sell tickets for a concert to people from places as far flung as California and Germany.

One CI web page for a small Midwestern suburb noticed persistent hits from Web users in Germany. Eventually they discovered the source of these hits: many young people from the area served in the army and were stationed in Germany, and these soldiers visited the local website to keep updated on news from home.

Digital-Divide Barriers Reduced

Electronic CI can play an important role in filling in the gaps between information "haves" and "have-nots." A CN with a public library connection provides public-access computers and builds capacity among non-profit organizations that serve low-income residents, at-risk groups, and people with disabilities. These are among the groups who often encounter barriers in accessing computers and the Internet. In these cases, CI can make a difference.

> A municipal health-department official who, due to the wide-ranging information that the CN provides at no cost via public libraries, asserted that it "is the single greatest opportunity of access for minorities."

> An employee at a non-profit noted that "many of the people we serve are the least likely to have their own computers and Internet access. The CN allows access to everyone through dial-up services and public-library access."

> An agency that serves a disabled community has created an online access guide to its city, which appears on their CN-sponsored page. The guide offers information on access to parking, buildings, restrooms, telephones, water fountains, and so on, provided by local businesses to persons with disabilities.

Reluctance to Seek Information or Communicate Reduced

Some people appear to be unwilling or unable to ask sensitive questions and prefer the anonymity provided by the Internet. CNs therefore increase their ability to seek information on the Web or ask questions via the Internet. In particular, organizations report having witnessed a surge in the amount of feedback and anonymous inquiries they receive as well as an increase in their ability to respond to requests.

> A local police chief says that he has seen an increase in the number of inquiries his department receives from citizens. He suspects that this is due to the fact that people are more likely to turn to the police for help if given the opportunity to interact with the department anonymously online.

> The staff at an AIDS organization realizes that people with HIV disease are still sometimes the target of discrimination. Because of this, many people are afraid to seek help. Therefore, being able to anonymously contact the organization via email or access information on the Web has greatly increased the comfort level of the people the organization serves.

A staff member from a psychological counseling service also noted the increased sense of comfort that patrons get through anonymous Web inquiries: "Many of the people we serve see counseling and therapy as bad words. Even if they're in the midst of something difficult, they may be really uncomfortable stopping to talk about it. But if information is available on the Internet, they can find out what they need to know and where to go."

A Community Network Can Help to Increase the Effectiveness of Non-Profit Organizations and Help Them Be More Responsive to the Community

Service providers benefit from collaborating with CNs in several ways. Libraries help numerous community organizations, government agencies, and small businesses get their websites off the ground. One librarian we spoke to referred to this as "incubating" a website. Major benefits identified by IPs include: an ability to communicate more effectively with their clientele; an increased ability to serve their clientele effectively; an enhanced visibility; increased financial support; and a wider base of well-trained volunteers.

Save Community Organizations Time and Money

Time and money are two resources that non-profits and government agencies have in short supply. Through their participation in a CN, many organizations have realized impressive cost savings.

Regarding the free server space and training provided by the CN, one non-profit employee said, "It sounds too good to be true, but it is true."

A local historical society volunteer remarked on the decreased costs of making their organization's information available via the CN: "By having the Internet available, you don't necessarily reduce the mailing costs, but you can provide information in different ways. You can create a whole page about an event at no additional cost." While the group continues to spread its message with traditional media, such as hardcopy newsletters, they can now also provide more detailed information over the Internet at no additional cost.

According to one school-district employee: "What makes the CN successful is the way it is based on a network system. You already have that infrastructure in place so you're not building something from scratch—that would take forever. If you start it from the library, you can work from there and save a great deal of time in doing so."

"Our group put together a book for all of our third graders about the history of our town. It would cost quite a bit of money to print. I put it up on the Internet. Once you've put it online, it doesn't cost anything to have it there."

Increase Organizational Visibility

Traditional marketing media such as television and print advertising present costly barriers for non-profits to overcome. As a result, many have felt that some community members who needed their services simply did not know their work. IPs that work with their local CNs have found that the CN connection allows them to reach their target audiences effectively, and they have been able to present a complete picture of their organization while staying within the bounds of their budget.

In the past few years there have been a few studies and considerable debate on the effects of the Internet on people's communication. We saw evidence that the CN's linkages to the Internet enhanced the ability of local governments and non-profit organization service providers to communicate with their clientele and others. Organizations have experienced an increase in communication with clientele by way of email.

A volunteer at a local historical society noted a marked increase in communication since the organization posted its web pages on the CN. She said, "We are amazed at the way in which people from places throughout the country—and throughout the world—come and visit our page. We even get emails from people who had a connection to our community three generations ago."

A fireman who serves as his department's webmaster said this about the increase in communication as a result of their web page: "Because we have a presence on the Internet, there are people thinking, 'If they have a web page, maybe they'll be nice enough to answer my email.' So we get emails from all over the world."

A representative from a Little League baseball team said that since he posted a club web page on the CN, he has been flooded with emails from parents of the players. He uses this feedback to inform the club's board members of parents' concerns and questions.

One community member is involved in a print exchange for wood-block carvers. After learning of the CN from a librarian, he designed a web page for the CN that allows woodblock printers from all over the world to share their prints and exchange information about techniques, inks, and tools of the trade.

A health-oriented foundation cited the "tremendous reach" possible due to their new website.

A veterans' association member believes that having a website has helped his organization promote a more positive image of the organization and "defy the stereotype of a bunch of old guys sitting around." The organization does quite a bit of community service, and a number of the members volunteer at the local school. The Web allows them an opportunity to alert the citizens to their community involvement.

A representative of a large, national non-profit organization noted that having a presence on the CN gives his local chapter a voice. Many community residents are aware of the organization, he said, yet few understand what the non-profit has done for the local community. This way, the local chapter can inform their community of exactly the types of activities the organization invests in locally. In their case, they alert their constituents to their efforts to help families and support local education initiatives.

Increased Responsiveness to the Community

Increased communication between organizations and the clientele results in greater responsiveness by agencies to the people they serve. The interactive nature of the Internet allows for quicker response time and more frequent information updates. Organizations also indicated that technology enables them to better serve their clientele.

According to one fireman, his local CN is a tool for making government more responsive and approachable. He receives a variety of information requests via email and makes fire-safety information available online so citizens can locate answers to their questions more easily.

One city official has taken an active role in his CN because he feels information technology can make government more responsive to its citizens, especially due to the interactive nature of the Web. In fact, he goes so far as to assert that citizens have a right to feel angry with government that doesn't make government information available online.

A radio station for the visually impaired has started to make its programs available on demand via Real Audio streaming on their CN web page. The station's director views technology as a way to give "blind drivers a lane on the information superhighway." He notes that his group is ahead of the curve because reading services in other locations do not have web pages, email boxes, or streaming audio.

Organizations now have the potential to offer their clientele information twenty-four hours a day, seven days a week via the Internet. This can represent a tremendous advantage, especially for someone in need. As one social-service-agency-employee points out, "Many times people are in crisis in the middle of the night, and they don't know where to turn. And so we thought, 'Boy, if we could have a website where people could fill in an intake form so that in the morning it's there, and somebody can call and set up an appointment immediately, it would be a real service.'"

A Community Network Can Increase the Ability to Access Relevant Information

People reported an increased ability to access relevant CI. Our interviews with users of CNs repeatedly revealed the appreciation that people felt being able to get information that they had previously viewed as hard to get. They told us that through the CN they felt that they were able to access a "higher quality" of information—more current, more comprehensive, better organized, and linked to other relevant sources and sites. Users also found that the information brought together on the CN was easier to use. That saved them time, money, and energy, reducing their "transaction costs" and increasing the convenience of getting information. Finally, CN users felt that they had an increased ability to identify trusted information.

Groups Value Organized Information

Librarians' skills in organizing CI resources span several decades. As a result, CNs sponsored by libraries reflected these skills. Our study showed that service providers recognized and were able to benefit from the CN's well-organized information.

One IP noted the contrast between the thoughtfully organized library-sponsored CN and other community websites that seemed to have no rhyme or reason regarding how things are listed on the page. The subject-based organizational scheme at her CN enables her users to save time wading through all the information online.

A government official from a large county noted that keeping track of "who's who" in government is a tricky proposition, but that the CN offers well-organized links to government information.

Unbiased/Neutral/Trusted Information Sources Are Valued

For all of the benefits of the Internet, nagging concerns regarding the trustworthiness of online information still haunt many users. People want assurances that the information they access is non-biased. With this in mind, IPs can see the benefit of CI that comes from a trusted local source. Librarians and libraries are seen as unbiased sources of information.

One IP expressed the concept of trust in the following way: "I would say the library contact is the best part of our connection with the community network. Putting the library in that role is the biggest benefit to the community and the library."

Another IP referred to the advantage working with the library brings to their organization: "I think that one of the benefits of partnering with the library is that the library's constituency is everyone. No one is left out. The library represents all points of view. It's content neutral. All IPs want to appeal to the entire general public, and being connected with the library makes this possible."

A Community Network Can Help Community Groups Become Information Providers and Value Librarians' Knowledge and Values

Non-profit organizations have largely viewed themselves as service providers rather than IPs. Many service providers have placed only modest emphasis on the valuable information their organizations have to offer. Moreover, in the past, little consideration went into evaluating how individuals were supposed to find out about non-profit services. Word of mouth was often viewed as the most reliable method to learn about an organization's programs. Today, however, the Internet has dramatically changed the ways in which individuals find information.

Very importantly, CNs help non-profits and government agencies become *information providers*. The CNs we studied have actively worked with organizations in their communities to help them become IPs. As IPs, these non-profits and government agencies are learning to recognize their responsibility to provide content regarding their services and programs via their library-sponsored electronic CNs. The non-profit organizations we interviewed have come to recognize the tremendous potential of information sharing and collaboration through their CN. In the process, groups become more likely to link to and from related information, understand the value of information currency for their own information and that of others, and come to value librarians' knowledge, skills, and ability to increase access to CI. Examples of the use of two valuable tools for IPs are shown below.

Groups Begin to Link to and from Related Information

Involvement in the CN has helped community organizations realize the importance of linking to relevant websites; hyperlinking gives people immediate access to related information resources. The CNs we re-searched encouraged IPs to link to relevant information and modeled this behavior by providing websites that set the example for the communities they serve. Hyperlinking is a key component of virtual community.

> A local non-profit organization that serves the disabled indicates that it is essential that they have a web page because they are affiliated with a national group, and the organization's national site refers people to local chapters through Internet links.

> A school-district representative told us of the benefit the CN has in strengthening the links among local organizations, both virtually and physically. She says that by having a website on the network, "we are part of that community, not just some name off the Web with nothing surrounding or relating to us. We are embedded in the community."

Groups Understand the Value of Providing Current Information

Because maintenance of Web documents often requires less work than updating traditional printed materials, disseminating information online can be a sensible alternative for many time- and money-strapped organizations. The CN has helped IPs appreciate the value of current information, including their own and that of other non-profits as well. Here are examples of people we encountered over the course of our study who realized the benefits of currency:

> One association volunteer told us about an instance in which the date of a flower show his organization was sponsoring was incorrectly printed in the group's newsletter. He asked: "How do you let the audience know? You can change the website, but you're not going to redo a newsletter mailing." It was easy for him to revise the website to reflect the correct date for the event. He pointed out how far less time and money were required for the online update.

> Thanks to the CN, a village trustee now posts the town meeting minutes online within a day or two of the meeting to alert citizens to issues discussed by the board. Previously this public information wasn't available to the community until weeks—sometimes months—after a meeting.

Organizations Learn to Become Information Providers, and the Community Benefits

In the process of becoming IPs, groups learn to value organized information, they begin to link to and from related information resources, and they come to appreciate unbiased, neutral, or trusted sources of information. Our findings indicate that many have learned to value the work of librarians and even to think like librarians. When non-profit organizations see themselves as IPs they are likely to assume the responsibility of increasing the access of their constituents to information. This puts librarians in a leadership role in increasing access to CI.

The quotations below, from citizens of the three case-study communities, indicate the value they place on the CN as a one-stop shopping place that brings the community together. These comments would be impossible without the participation of a critical mass of IPs who contribute their relevant information.

> This site contains a wealth of information specific to the metro area and is one of my favorites.

> It brings everything to one location. It's very easy to navigate around in, and everything is right there at your fingertips—it's just right there.

> I absolutely rely on this website for home and work projects. I also refer lots of people I speak to, from both out of state and locally,

to the website. It cuts through all the garbage and gets straight to the heart!

The CN is really the best place to go to find out about jobs—all the information is right there. You can find out about benefits, the salary—all on the website.

A Community Network Can Contribute to Community Building, Foster Civic Engagement, and Create a Sense of Community

CNs are designed to build community. They do it in a number of ways. The Westat study of the impact of 1994–1996 NTIA-funded projects identified a number of potential community outcomes of technology projects (that included, but were not limited to, CNs). They asked respondents to indicate the extent to which their projects achieved these outcomes.

> The most commonly cited community outcomes were improving training opportunities, enhancing long-term telecommunication needs, coordinating community-wide communication services, and enhancing community development (2000).

Our CN profiles provide examples of the ways in which CNs foster these kinds of community-building outcomes. Our study used qualitative approaches and extrapolated benefits based on our site visits. It is clear to us that the types of community outcomes identified certainly were present in the CNs we examined.

Bringing Organizations Together

According to an old cliché, the whole is often greater than the sum of its parts. The well-designed CNs we examined develop mechanisms including electronic discussion lists, community meetings, marketing, and outreach activities designed to assure that IPs see themselves as part of a larger community.

> An employee at a non-profit that serves AIDS patients indicates that the CN works as a catalyst that links his organization with other like-minded groups: "AIDS services are often fragmented, leaving people who are living with HIV infection wondering where to

turn. Having our website hosted on the network allows us to pool our resources and create links to other agencies, thus broadening the availability of resources."

A representative from a local cable-access station spoke of network benefits in the following way: "We've found being involved in a local network is a great feature. Other people are here; they are people like you and a good representation of your community. It's better than hanging out there by yourself."

One IP shared these insights on the power of social networking: "The idea that I'm part of this larger thing, and you can get my information, but you can also get information on other organizations. For example, if I am the yoga teacher in town, maybe I'll link to other community network sites that relate to health and fitness, or maybe I'll link back to my community site. As a result, there's much more of value on my website than just my yoga information."

Fostering Idea Sharing

CNs break down natural barriers that keep groups apart including the lack of trust of individuals and groups who fall outside of the daily existence. In addition, people from government agencies and non-profits have decidedly busy schedules. CNs foster idea sharing in a variety of ways; they offer a forum for organizations to communicate, and, therefore, to be able to share ideas and resources.

One CN participant described the atmosphere at a recent meeting of CN participants: "I was sitting there in a room with people representing pretty much every facet of a community. You had a business owner, a fireman, a police officer, as well as people representing a social-service agency, the chamber of commerce, school districts, and park districts. That's what I think is the coolest idea—the PTA president and the police chief might get together, the park district and someone who works with physically disabled kids might get together, the school librarian and the public librarian might get together."

A parks and recreation employee sits on an advisory committee for her CN. She says her responsibility on the committee results in serendipitous benefits. The members use these meetings as an opportunity to share ideas with other community representatives.

Strengthening Organizational Partnerships

Collaboration builds on increased trust and idea sharing among organizations. We have ample evidence that librarians involved in CNs actively work to increase collaboration in their communities. Strong organizational partnerships contribute to community building. The CNs that we examined used the Internet and interpersonal communication to increase the communication among organizations, as a prerequisite to increased collaboration.

> A police department partners with the local library to offer an Internet-safety program. The officers say that since their department developed a website, the use of the Internet as an interactive communication tool has greatly enhanced community-policing efforts. A librarian talked about the authority that partnership with the police department lends to their collaboration efforts: "For me to bring in a uniformed representative from the local police department adds an incredible amount of credibility to our workshop on Internet safety. The CN makes a difference in our community by bringing together groups of people and organizations within the community that might not otherwise have an opportunity to interact."
>
> One small-town library spoke of the direct increase in collaboration as a result of their central involvement in the CN. Since beginning involvement, the library has signed off on two collaborative grant applications, one with the high school and another with the senior center.

Increasing Training Opportunities and Telecommunication Capabilities

The federal government's study of the effectiveness of federally funded technology projects found that the most common community improvements as the result of TIIAP-funded projects were improved training opportunities and enhancement of telecommunication use and capability (Westat 2000).

Our study found that the case study CNs both increased the training opportunities in their communities and enhanced the telecommunication capabilities of very important community IPs who had found themselves on the wrong side of the digital divide. Providing these opportunities influenced the effectiveness of community organizations as service and information providers.

A village employee who developed a website with help from the library described the benefits in the following way: "The fact that it was available locally. There were people that you could go to— you can pick up the phone and say: 'Hey, I've got a problem.' What's more, you can get answers quickly. It's a great resource."

An IP who developed websites for a number of community organizations praised the assistance he received from his local library when he lacked the technical and organizational skills needed to develop community websites: "It's the personnel who are so important. I went to the library and talked to my contact there. I didn't have a clue, and he took me by the hand, and I think it was two months before I went online. Not only did he show me, but also he explained what a website is, and why a site would be good for my organization and to the community."

Another individual who worked in a very small non-profit organization said: "I wanted to learn the mechanics of building and maintaining a site. The hands-on experience I got from working with the network gives me more control over the content of our website. When you go through a design firm you have to try to explain to them how to represent you, but when you do it yourself, you can get it right faster."

A local non-profit told us how the network staff has been very helpful in getting them started by providing great technical assistance and a volunteer, who created their first page. Additionally, the CN staff and volunteers have built a network of social-service providers that greatly improves communication possibilities.

One school employee talked about how the library helped "incubate" their first web pages. Since that time, the site grew so much that the school eventually had to get its own Web server. In the process of working with the library, school staff gained enough Web expertise to launch their own site.

Civic Engagement through Increased Volunteerism and Support

The raison d'etre of community non-profit organizations is to reach out to serve the community. Most well-functioning non-profit organizations work to harness the energies of volunteers to serve their clientele. The CN offers IPs a potent recruiting tool both for volunteers and support. Volunteerism is one component of civic engagement. Again, we have evidence that CNs may foster civic engagement.

> An organization that provides special services to the elderly finds that its website helps recruit new clientele, while keeping their current audience better informed of its offerings. The website also serves as an effective recruitment tool for the organization, which now boasts close to three hundred volunteers.

> A representative from an agency that supports single, low-income parents said, "We have been asked about opening a new childcare center. In addition, people are offering to volunteer and sponsor a fundraising event for us" due to increased public awareness created by the website.

> One local non-profit shared this story: "A woman looking for travel information about our city ended up on our CN site. She looked at the non-profit wish list posted on the CN and read our request for items such as games, art supplies, and magazine subscriptions for middle school youth. Three days later, we received a large box full of board games, cards, puzzles, books, and an 8-bit Nintendo system and about fifty games!"

> For a municipal health department, the CN strengthens its grant-making activities. "Since funders often require that you show how you will share information on your activities with the community, [we] list the CN in our grant applications, citing the network as an important means of disseminating our message."

An Increased Sense of Community

Information sharing and collaboration result in greater knowledge of what's really happening in a community. CNs present a new avenue for IPs not only to share information about their organizations but also to gain a big picture view of the community. These actions will serve to build an increased sense of community. While laudable, this goal is hard to achieve. Only a minority of federally funded TOP projects succeeded in increasing a sense of community (Westat 2000). We saw evidence that librarians were contributing to an increased sense of community through the three CNs we studied closely.

> An IP in one community acknowledged that being part of a CN brought out a healthy spirit of competitiveness: "We meet and talk

about how many hits, how well you're doing, and the frustrations of making pages. And we put a little bit of pressure on each other—a little competitive pressure, so that our sites are kept up to date as much as we can, in the process we learn more about each other."

The village trustee of one community embraced the CN idea. She posted the village trustee agenda online so that citizens could see what issues were on the table. In response, groups told her that they were now much more aware of what was going on in the different areas of local politics and government.

A woman from California who was relocating to suburban Chicago used the CN to get a sense for the different communities in the area. One community's page caught her eye, and so she wrote to them: "Just from your website I think I'd like your community. What else can you tell me about it?"

The Benefits of Networked Community Information

In this research we identified potential benefits of networked CI. While these are not exhaustive, they provide powerful indicators of the range of impact. Likewise, we did not measure the extent to which they occur throughout the community. Nonetheless, throughout this chapter we have provided best-practice examples of how networked CI helps real people and organizations and how CNs provide incredible value for service providers, their clientele, and the community. Through our study of CI librarians we identified benefits of networked CI to individuals, their families, their neighborhoods, and the larger community. Because of what we learned both from CI librarians and from the CN case studies, we want to underscore that individuals make a distinction between getting information about the community and linking information to people. With that in mind, librarians and other facilitators of networked CI need to take more care in making sure that such information is not buried.

Our case studies of CNs yielded rich and convincing examples of how a CN can help a community through the information it brings together and the community-building activities that occur along the way. We divided the benefits of a CN into six broad categories that were further divided into their component parts. We saw that CNs are able to *over-*

come *barriers* that citizens had identified—including geographical and digital-divide barriers and the reluctance to ask for sensitive information. We found that the non-profit organizations we interviewed were able to articulate how the CN had served to increase their *effectiveness* by saving them time and money and increasing their knowledge, skill, and organizational visibility not only in the community but also beyond its borders. As a result of their increased effectiveness, these service providers found that they had been able to build capacity, becoming *more responsive* to their constituents and to the community.

In an earlier chapter we showed that people encounter barriers in the course of trying to get information—experiencing information overload, irrelevance, problems in determining what information to trust, lack of understanding of the Web, and lack of confidence in their abilities to use this technology. CNs, we found, *increase the ability to access relevant information* thus empowering community organizations to provide their clientele with well-organized, trusted information sources brought together in the CN. Very importantly, CNs help non-profits and government agencies become *information providers*. In the process, groups become more likely to link to and from related information, understand the value of information currency for their own information and that of others, and come to value librarians' knowledge, skills, abilities, and their ability to increase access to CI.

The benefits of CNs summarized above have multiplier effects. A viable CN results in a critical mass of organizations that understand its functions and contribute to its success. When these conditions occur the CN can make strong contributions to *community building* by bringing organizations together, strengthening organizational partnerships, often resulting in increased training opportunities, organizational telecommunication capabilities, and other benefits. A CN can foster civic engagement through volunteerism and other means, and it can create among the citizens a sense of community.

In spite of our findings showing the wide range of impacts of networked CI, currently librarians lack adequate evaluation tools for determining the effectiveness of their initiatives in community building and their contributions to bridging the digital divide. Our findings on the benefits of networked CI and CNs can be used to develop the needed context-centered tools and approaches that can systematize the collection of data about how information is used by people and groups. We will discuss this in the next chapter devoted to the evaluation challenge.

5

Best Practices

Public Libraries, Community Information, and Community Networking

This chapter answers the question: What "best practices" for library and service provider participation in community networking and Internet CI access can be identified that will benefit other libraries and communities?

The identification of best practices in CI provision was an important part of our research. During the course of our study, starting with the national survey of CI practice and continuing with proactive searches for CI best practice, we collected numerous examples of best practices in CI provision. As time went on, categories of CI best practices emerged. Therefore, we created a section devoted to highlighting libraries that offer model CI services (see http://www.si.umich.edu/helpseek/bestpractices/). Several of the examples have been discussed in chapter 3, such as CI databases, digitized collections, GIS, and digital reference. However, we identified many other examples of CI best practices.

The categories of best practice in CI include:

Access issues/digital divide

CI services

Interactive CI or CN features

Specialized content

Agency/local government content

Partnerships

Training

The best practices below merely reflect a sample of the examples for the different categories. For more examples, please see our website at http://www.si.umich.edu/helpseek/bestpractices/. Each category is briefly described above the examples for that category.

Access Issues and the Digital Divide

In this digital age, public libraries are making a special effort to provide information access to underserved populations by offering free Internet access and, in some cases, free email accounts. Librarians are also organizing information with particular target populations in mind, such as the homeless, immigrants, or special-needs populations. The following libraries target underserved populations in their CI provision.

Queens Borough Public Library

http://www.queenslibrary.org/

With an ethnically diverse population representing more than 120 countries and 100 languages, it is not surprising that the Queens Borough Public Library devotes a great deal of attention to reaching out to recent immigrants and non-native English speakers. The Queens Borough Public Library website includes a variety of foreign-language resources and a directory of immigrant-serving agencies. In fact, the Queens Directory of Immigrant-Serving Agencies is a centerpiece of the library website and the fruit of the librarians' extensive connections with Queens' community organizations. Librarians compiled this massive searchable database of organizations offering services to immigrants in more than fifty languages. Organizations in the database offer everything from academic counseling to substance-abuse counseling to disabled transportation. The directory is available in print as well, and it is a wonderful example of how, with some database knowledge and the right connections with the community, a library can manage to publish an entire reference work.

Kansas City Public Library Cultural Mosaic

http://www.kclibrary.org/cultural/

The library's efforts to bridge the digital divide are evident on the library's community pages. "Cultural Mosaic" is a directory of relevant websites and library resources for African Americans, Latinos, women, seniors, and so on. This rich directory aggregates related information resources with helpful annotations. These pages are specifically directed at traditionally underserved populations. For example, the library's Native American resources include links to cultural heritage sites, Native American health pages, tribal events calendars, and relevant literature.

Suncoast Free-Net

http://www.scfn.net/

The Suncoast Free-Net (SCFN) is sponsored and maintained by the Tampa-Hillsborough Public Library System. The SCFN says that its mission is to provide the public with a wide range of easily accessible and useful information. Librarians and free-net volunteers update the content of the site frequently. In an effort to enhance communication, the SCFN offers a free, community-oriented telecomputing network for the Tampa Bay area. Computers with free-net access are available at all Pinellas and Hillsborough libraries. In addition, SCFN provides free email addresses for its registered users, and in the last few years, SCFN has had a steady number of about 10,000 registered users. A recent article in the *St. Petersburgh Times* noted the value of the free-net's effort to bridge the digital divide: "The Suncoast Free-Net remains one of the original and most popular ways for the poor, and the poorly equipped, to have equal access to information."

Community Information Services

Public libraries have, as we have discussed, converted CI files into digital formats. The following examples showcase several digital CI services. We discovered several libraries that offer specialized local information services. Although the specific nature of these services varies, the libraries are similar in the fact that each of these libraries highlights their special CI service. While some libraries have pooled resources within their system or with partner community organizations to create a CN, other libraries have fostered the growth of a CI service out of what may have started as a CI database or telephone I&R service.

Fort Worth Public Library CORE (Community Resources)

http://www.fortworthlibrary.org/core.htm/

The Fort Worth Public Library won a Department of Justice grant to fund their CI program, called CORE for COmmunity REsources. In its beginning, CORE was a database created to serve at-risk youth and their families; however, it has evolved into a much more comprehensive file. Information for finding help with housing, healthcare, food banks, runaway assistance, shelters and job training now shares space with information on local clubs and organizations. The database has become a one-stop source for all quality of life needs. Approximately 2,500 Tarrant County organizations are described in the database. Information for each includes telephone numbers, locations, bus routes, hours of service, and eligibility. The listings are searchable by name, keyword, or subject. The database itself is currently available through the library catalog section of the library homepage (click on community resources). All library personnel are trained to help users search CORE. The CORE database is also available at CORE workstations, which have been placed in key city, community, and recreation centers. Plans are currently underway to enhance the effectiveness of the service at these sites. CORE team members visit these and teach database searching techniques to center staff.

North Suburban Library System and Suburban Library System

http://www.northstarnet.org/

The NorthStarNet (NSN) CN, a partnership between the North Suburban Library System (NSLS) and Suburban Library Systems (SLS), is designed to help bring Chicago's suburban communities together in virtual space even though they are dispersed in physical space. NSN represents 62 libraries in 118 Chicago-area communities. The CN provides free hosting and technical support to local organizations, small businesses, government agencies, and community groups. Content decisions are made locally and are responsive to the information needs of each particular community. NSN exhibits an annotated listing of helpful local resources in its regional resources pages. Topics covered range from education—which includes K–12, financial aid, and higher education—to arts, culture, and entertainment. Users can also identify local resources by matching a subject area, such as social services or business, with the name of their community on the Chicagoland Local Information search page.

York County Library System FIRST

http://www.1st.org/

Free Information and Referral System Teleline (FIRST) is a patron's FIRST stop for Information about York County (PA). FIRST represents the result of a partnership between the York County Library System, the United Way of York County and the County of York. This web- and telephone-referral resource lists more than one thousand non-profit services as well as hundreds of programs and events throughout York County. FIRST is proud of the fact that they respond to thirty thousand information requests a year. Inquiries range in need from food, shelter, and clothing to consumer issues, legal needs, health, and employment questions.

Interactive Community Information or Community Network Features

As technology improves and user demands increase, interactivity of websites has become a major feature in many electronic resources. Therefore, it comes as little surprise that those libraries that are leading the way in CI provision are also beginning to offer interactive features on their library websites. Examples of interactivity include downloadable government applications, online reference, submission and feedback forms, and online tutorial help, where the focus is the convenience of the user.

Houston Public Library Online Interactive Reference Services

http://www.hpl.lib.tx.us/hpl/interactive/eref_form.html/

The Houston Public Library (HPL) now offers reference service through easy-to-use email-submission forms. With the Email Reference Form, brief questions are answered, or suggestions on sources and locations are offered to help find answers to more lengthy questions. Responses are provided within 36–48 hours or less, excluding weekends. Additionally, the Email Shelf Check Form allows patrons to ask HPL staff to check the shelves for a particular book, CD, tape, or other type of item. If the item is in the library at the time of the request, an online request can be made to send it to the HPL location of the user's choice. A librarian will also notify patrons of the status of the requested item by email.

CascadeLink

http://www.cascadelink.org/index.html/

The Multnomah County library offers online CI for people living in the Portland, Oregon–Vancouver–Washington region. CascadeLink is organized by subject and includes topics such as neighborhoods, jobs, arts and entertainment, and elections, among others. Users of CascadeLink are encouraged to update information through a series of dynamic web forms. One result of this interactive capability is the electronic community calendar. Indeed, CascadeLink features the most widely used and standardized community calendar for the region. CascadeLink also links to the library's community organization database (COOL) with listings of more than 5,500 organizations from throughout Oregon and southwest Washington.

Boston Public Library Online Tutoring Program

http://www.bpl.org/

In addition to the wide variety of traditional programs, the Boston Public Library offers an online tutoring project to reach out to the local communities. It is an extension of their (in-person) Homework Assistance Program. The pilot program is targeting Boston middle school and high school students, particularly in standardized-testing assistance. Students and their tutors access the online environment through the use of a password.

Specialized Content

We saw many cases in which librarians developed specialized content for their library's website. The creation of locally relevant and purposely aggregated materials is not new to the CI field. However, the migration of this content to the Web presents an opportunity for the library to have a greater impact. Now clientele can access this information twenty-four hours a day, seven days a week. Following are some examples of locally created materials regarding everything from economic development to education.

Pasadena Public Library Neighborhood Profiles

http://www.ci.pasadena.ca.us/library/profiles.asp/

With the Pasadena Public Library website's Neighborhood Profiles feature, users can find out more about any Pasadena neighborhood with a library branch. Each profile includes a brief history of the neighborhood as well as demographic information, and listings of political districts, local schools, and neighborhood associations. In addition, Neighborhood Profiles offers a clickable map interface that makes it easy for patrons to locate the library branch nearest them.

Skokie Public Library, Skokie Community

http://www.skokie.lib.il.us/

There are several resources available here on the Skokie Community website, such as the official websites of the village of Skokie and its chamber of commerce and an online index to Skokie newspapers. More robust is the library-sponsored SkokieNet (http://www.skokienet.org/index.html/), which features a range of browsable categories, from social services to restaurants to businesses. In terms of specific CI, there is a community calendar, a list of local non-profit agencies, a collection on local history, and a section of demographic information, as well as a section on currently pending local issues. Each category provides an extensive list of organizations, often further categorized. In all, this site provides high-quality information about a wide range of community activities, organizations, and opportunities.

Three Rivers Free-Net (TRFN)

http://trfn.clpgh.org/

The Carnegie Library of Pittsburgh's TRFN displays an impressive annotated collection of local, state, and national economic development resources. The Pittsburgh listings are particularly strong and cover topics ranging from current urban development projects to small-business venture-capital funding. TRFN's thoughtful organization scheme is also evident in its social-services area. Here users can access social-service information in a variety of ways including by organization name, type of service, or by population served. The selected hotlines directory is particularly helpful for users seeking resources in emergency situations. TRFN's subject coverage is equally extensive in a variety of other areas such as education, employment, transportation, and health issues. Please refer to the TRFN's Subject Guide for more information.

Local Government Agency Content

We discovered numerous examples of communities in which local government agencies had teamed up with the library to provide government information via the library web pages. In some cases, the library even hosted the county or city website. These represent examples of how partnership among city agencies can leverage the CI resources to make more information available to a larger population. Such online government features make considerable strides in informing citizens and encouraging civic participation

Baltimore County Public Library

http://www.bcplonline.org/

The Baltimore County Public Library has an Election, Voting, and Politics page with information on voter registration, the election calendar, election results, FAQs, and so on. The library developed many of the pages, while others are from the government or interest groups.

Hartford Public Library

http://www.hartfordpl.lib.ct.us/

Special to this site is a section devoted to the city's Charter Review Commission, which includes minutes, agendas, commissioners, and even discussion lists—cyber democracy in action! These and other pages keep the library's website "live," with current and changing information. For instance, during tax season 2000, an easy-to-spot front-page link brings users tax forms and information on getting tax help at the library. Right on the front page are links to Hispanic Resources on the Web and Black History on the Web. The CI database is very broad (from "cemeteries" to keyword-searchable city council meeting minutes), with a very simple interface.

Seattle Public Library

http://www.spl.org/

The Seattle Public Library provides a directory of online municipal codes from cities all over the country, one of the most comprehensive municipal-code collections on the Web. If you've ever wanted to compare your city's laws to other cities, the Seattle Public Library website is for you. It also has an elaborate directory of items related to local, county, state, and federal government.

Partnerships

Among the most powerful examples of CI provision we came across were found among those libraries involved in community partnerships. We saw that collaborative efforts to enhance community took various forms, but when community organizations, government agencies, and even businesses partnered with the library, the community benefited. The pooling of local resources and investment of community stakeholders often makes for a sustainable and strong CI service.

Tallahassee Freenet

http://www.tfn.net/

The Tallahassee Freenet (TFN), Florida's first CN and one of the nation's first library-CN partnerships, was started in 1993 by faculty from Florida State University (FSU). Early on, the LeRoy Collins Leon County Public Library joined as an operating partner. Over time partners have changed, but the public library has continued to be a primary stakeholder. TFN has ties to county government, state government, the universities, the newspaper, hospitals, and hundreds of community organizations. TFN seeks to serve as "a catalyst for the educational, social, and economic growth of Tallahassee, Leon County, and Florida through online community networking." They do this through involving community businesses and individuals as supporters, partners, and volunteers who serve in a variety of capacities including acting as editors of content web pages.

Minuteman Library Network

http://www.mln.lib.ma.us/index2.htm/

Libraries frequently collaborate with one another as consortia to take advantage of the economies of scale in the delivery of bibliographic services. This sort of arrangement can also result in effective ways of providing CI to citizens. Massachusetts' Minuteman Library Network is a good example of this powerful trend. There are thirty-eight libraries (thirty-four public and four academic) in the Minuteman system. The network oversees the development and maintenance of the Community Information and Referral File, which lists more than 2,500 local agencies and organizations. This searchable database provides contact information and descriptions of services as well as notes regarding area served, languages spoken, facilities, directions, and, when appropriate, website links.

Hancock County Community Network

http://www.hccn.org/

The Hancock County Community Network (HCCN) is a regional information source sponsored by the Hancock County Public Library (IN). The library works in cooperation with several other private and public organizations to bring CI to the people of Hancock County. The site features demographic data for ten different communities, along with links to government agencies, community organizations, businesses, healthcare facilities, and educational institutions. This CN encourages interactivity. For example, citizens can post their concerns on the community bulletin board, suggest a link, or advertise an upcoming event on the community calendar.

Michiana Free-Net

http://michiana.org/MFNetMainMenu.html/

The St. Joseph County Public Library in collaboration with MCI, Notre Dame University, and NAPnet brings the Michiana Free-Net to St. Joseph, Indiana. The Michiana Free-Net was the first free-net of its type in Indiana having been founded back in August 1994.

The free-net offers a rich directory of local information, which includes links to community organizations and clubs, area businesses, government information, educational institutions, and religious organizations, among others. The free-net continues to offer Internet connections to the community based on a sliding-scale payment system. For a small additional fee, Michiana Free-Net also provides server space for business, organization, and personal web pages. Small non-profits are eligible to have this fee waived.

Training

Training is a critical piece in the adoption of any new technology. More and more libraries now offer computer and Internet skills building through public classes. Instruction at public libraries ranges from basic computer skills to advanced training in the use of specialized content. As mentors and trainers, librarians find themselves directing their clientele to CI. Therefore, technology training at public libraries often goes hand in hand with a strong electronic CI service.

The Ela Area Public Library, Library Events

http://www.ela.alibrary.com/

The Ela Area Public Library provides its community with a rich array of electronic resource training classes. The library's Internet Reference Specialist teaches classes ranging from beginners' seminars, such as a hands-on introduction to the Web, to more advanced training sessions (e.g., designing websites for small businesses). Not only does this hands-on training acquaint users with the Web at large, special emphasis is placed on the library's CI files. Yet another class offered is "Window into Time," a session that encourages residents to add their family photos and documents to a local online history exhibit.

Multnomah County Library, Library Events and Classes

http://www.multnomah.lib.or.us/lib/events/classes/

The Multnomah County Library offers classes on topics as varied as basic Web searching, conducting investment research, developing job-searching skills, and gaining consumer smarts. Use of the Internet is integrated into each of these classes. In addition, the library encourages families to participate in Cyber-Sundays on Sunday afternoons, a time when the entire family can benefit from one-on-one help browsing the Web, playing educational CD-ROM games, looking up books, or conducting in-depth research.

FairNet

http://www.fairnet.org/

FairNet serves residents of interior Alaska. This CN represents a partnership between the Fairbanks North Star Borough Public Library, Rasmuson Library Computing and Communications, the Fairbanks North Star Borough (FNSB) School District, KUAC Radio, and the United Way Volunteer Action Center. FairNet's mission is to be the community clearinghouse of information serving Fairbanks and the surrounding area.

FairNet provides free public access points to FairNet and the Internet, content about community activities, events and points of interest, and free dial-in access to FairNet and the Internet. In addition to information, access, and content, FairNet is helping the community address their information technology needs through services that include:

Training in basic computer use and the Internet

Promotion of the FNSB and interior Alaska to the world

Free Internet access to all residents of the borough

Homepage development and presence on the Internet

The New York Public Library, the Branch Libraries: CHOICES in Health Information

http://www.nypl.org/branch/health/

Through their program CHOICES, the New York Public Library branch libraries provide access to up-to-date health information on a wide range of topics including diseases, medications and medical tests, pregnancy and childcare, wellness and prevention, alternative medicine, how to find a physician, aging and geriatrics, healthcare costs and quality, mental health, AIDS, and HIV. In addition to books, videos, and periodicals, the library also provides free Internet access to full-text health information. Internet and basic health reference sources are available in all branch libraries. The library also provides free seventy-five-minute introductory workshops on how to search for health-related information, including how to evaluate online health information.

6

The Evaluation Challenge

This chapter focuses on the evaluation challenges faced by those who seek to effectively evaluate their services. It frames the answers to the project's evaluation research questions. Thus this chapter addresses the following questions:

What tools and processes do librarians require for evaluating the organizational impact of library-Internet access to CI and library participation in community networking?

What tools can be developed that will facilitate these best practices?

It builds particularly on the findings we presented in the chapters on benefits and best practice. We have shown that viewing networked CI, particularly CNs, from the perspective of those who benefit from it yields vital data for tool development. Our data shows that beneficiaries include individuals, community organizations, and the larger community. Individuals report a wide range of personal, family, and neighborhood benefits from networked CI. The three CNs were able to help community organizations overcome access barriers, become effective *information* providers while at the same time becoming more effective *service* providers, reach expanded audiences, engage in more partnerships, and become more responsive to the community. We also found that the cumulative benefits that CNs bring to community organizations result in benefits that accrue to the larger community.

The Evaluation Problem

In spite of the fact that our study has revealed a wide range of benefits identified by citizens and organization leaders themselves, at present librarians lack the tools they need to capture data on benefits or impact. Evaluation tools have steadily evolved for twenty years. Over time new tools have been developed to give librarians increasingly better ways to measure library performance. Current measures provide indicators of the extent to which library services reach the community; for example, librarians have been able to collect per capita data on circulation, reference questions, program attendance, and so on, for nearly two decades (Van House 1987). Recently Bertot et al. developed a manual that will help librarians measure networked services—an increasingly large part of what most librarians do (Bertot et al. 2001). That manual, based on extensive study of deployment and evaluation of networked services, identifies a candidate group of measures and guides librarians through the process of implementing them (2001). Likewise, Hernon and Altman's recent book on library evaluation encourages library staff to involve users in the evaluation of library services—a positive move (1998).

In spite of these advances, librarians are not yet able to determine the impact of library services on those who use them. Authors of a recent IMLS report declare that librarians need to ask, "What has changed as a result of our work?" (IMLS 2000) Our own study shows that most CI librarians are painfully aware that their current tools cannot help them answer this question. When asked the extent to which their current methods of evaluating the public's use of CI were effective, the overwhelming majority of CI librarians clearly saw them as ineffective (see figure 6.1).

We are not alone in our concern about librarians' inability to determine the value of library services. Peggy Rudd, director of the Texas State Library and Archives Commission, says: "Those of us who have committed our life's work to the improvement of libraries are continually frustrated with our lack of ability to effectively 'tell the library story.' While it would be much more convenient if the worth of libraries was simply accepted on faith by university presidents, county commissioners, city managers, and school boards, that is frequently not the case. Outcome measurement has the potential to be a powerful tool to help us substantiate the claims we know to be true about the impact of libraries in our institutions and in our society" (IMLS 2000).

FIGURE 6.1 PERCEPTIONS OF CURRENT EVALUATION APPROACHES

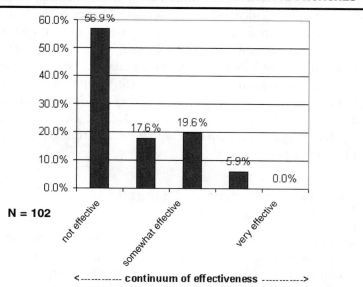

A community leader quoted by Bishop et al. underscores the need to determine outcomes:

> If you want to open the library's doors and be inviting to Black women, that means transforming the whole organization and how you do things. If the library wants to make sure it reaches members of that community, it needs to alter its relationships with them. Libraries should not just serve information; they should help build the community's capacity to create information (Bishop et al. 2000).

Jorge Schement has underscored the importance of understanding the context in which citizens seek information and adopt new technologies. He warned that libraries "lag in [their] understanding of the evolving social context—a context in which libraries will have to justify themselves," and suggested that libraries consider "how Americans [will] live their lives as citizens, as economic actors, and as social beings" (Benton Foundation and Libraries for the Future 1997).

Our research has shown that many CI librarians are already aware that CI can have an impact on the community. The problem, however, is that this knowledge is anecdotal and piecemeal, and no mechanism is in place to systematically gather it. The absence of such data prevents both citizens and CI librarians from communicating either the impact of CI or contributions or enhancements that CI makes to library services and missions. Without this information, librarians themselves remain uninformed about the outcomes of their own work in this area. As a consequence, managers have difficulty conducting informed analyses (e.g., to determine resource allocations, system improvements, etc.), miss opportunities to expand, improve important services, or build collaborations to increase the utilization of CI. Over time, a consistent lack of data about CI can negatively affect longer-term issues including future strategic decisions or decreased funding opportunities.

On the Horizon: A Changed Evaluation Environment

A convergence of several conditions has begun to influence the way professionals such as librarians think about evaluating their services. These include demands for public sector accountability coupled with an increased realization that current tools are inadequate, advances in scholarship and thus the emergence of viable models, and the recent commitment by governmental agencies to adopt new approaches designed to determine service impacts. These factors, taken together, could result in a greater acceptance of turning the mirror away from the institution and toward its clientele, more use of qualitative approaches to data collection, and the development of tools that have the capacity to determine the outcomes and impacts of service and resource use.

Demands for Public Sector Accountability

Interest in outcome and impact measures in the public sector is at an all-time high. There is a convergence of thought among decision makers that federal, state, and local governmental agencies, institutions, and non-profit organizations must begin to reshape their services and products to focus more effectively on outcomes. This has come as the result of loss of citizen confidence in the work of governmental agencies and recognition that current evaluation tools used by the public sector are inadequate.

For a decade the federal government has identified reinventing government as a priority and at the same time has focused on developing approaches government agencies can use to demonstrate results. Two federal initiatives in particular are driving interest in outcome measurement in governmental agencies: the Government Performance and Results Act (GPRA) of 1993, and the Government Accounting Standards Board Concepts Statement #2 in 1994 (Flynn 2000). These initiatives, which started at the federal level, are moving down to implementation at the local government level. "When GPRA is fully implemented, it will directly impact state and local governments that receive federal funding by requiring them to report on program results" (Flynn 2000).

Steps toward More Effective Evaluation Approaches through Scholarship

Michael Quinn Patton's definitive book on evaluation is a landmark contribution to understanding utilization-focused approaches to evaluation. It not only traces the development of these approaches, it also synthesizes many social-service evaluations and presents approaches to focusing a particular evaluation, evaluation questions, methods, data analysis, and presentation of findings (1997). Patton's hierarchy of evaluation puts measuring impact, or end results, at the top of the hierarchy (table 6.1).

TABLE 6.1   Patton's Hierarchy of Evaluation Criteria

End results	Measures of impact on overall problem, ultimate goals, side effects, social and economic consequences.
Practice and behavior change	Measures of adoption of new practices and behavior over time.
Knowledge, attitude, and skill change	Measures of individual and group changes in knowledge, attitudes, and skills.
Reactions	What participants and clients say about the program; satisfaction; interest, strengths, weaknesses.
Participation	The characteristics of program participants and clients; numbers; nature of involvement, background.
Activities	Implementation data on what the program actually offers.
Inputs	Resources expended; number and types of staff involved; time extended.

Note: From Patton (1997)

The W. K. Kellogg Foundation has recently issued its *Evaluation Handbook,* which is built on recent advances in evaluation scholarship. Developers of the handbook show those who receive foundation funding the importance of: examining how the project functions within the economic, social, and political environment of its community and project setting (context evaluation); using evaluation approaches in the process of planning, setting up, and carrying out of a project, as well as the documentation of the evolution of a project (implementation evaluation); and finally, assessing short- and long-term results of the project (outcome evaluation) (W. K. Kellogg Foundation 1998).

At the same time that scholarship in evaluation has focused more on outcomes, digital-library researchers in particular have examined the social aspects of the design, use, and impact of information systems (Bishop, in press).

Bishop and her colleagues argue that combining these approaches with participatory action research

> focuses digital library design and evaluation directly on the digital divide. Participatory action research demands relevant outcomes for marginalized members of society. It seeks to enhance the problem-solving capacities of local community members by actively involving them in every phase of research— from setting the problem to deciding how project outcomes will be assessed. In this approach, the intended users of a digital library participate as researchers, not subjects (Bishop et al. 2000).

Bishop and other researchers use scenarios developed by the target audience in the design of services and in their evaluation. They have found that "scenarios empower potential users as initiators in the analysis of information about their expectations and requirements, rather than treating them as mere informants in the design process" (Mehra 2000). Bishop et al. note that scenarios are needed to develop "a more complete picture of the social context of information-seeking and technology use for those marginalized groups who are often on the fringes of system design and evaluation" (2000).

The new evaluation approaches that have begun to be used by governmental agencies are far more likely to be more widely adopted because of the advances that have been made in the approaches to tool development. The attempts described below reflect tool development in its infancy. They do, however, show librarians and others in the public sector the kinds of activities that have been undertaken.

New Approaches by Governmental Agencies to Determine Impact

TIIAP

In its "comprehensive look at the impacts of the TIIAP investment" Westat (1999; 2000) sought to determine impact "in terms of the nature and degree of the effects on the organizations implementing the projects, other organizations that were involved with the projects, the individuals and communities that were served by the projects, and the specific value added by the TIIAP funds" (1999). In order to obtain this data, Westat developed broad evaluation questions, examined the awardees' grants and reports, conducted mail surveys, and developed case studies based on site visits. Community networks, Westat determined, were likely to: improve training and learning opportunities (59.9%); coordinate community-wide communication services (53.6%); and serve long-term telecommunication needs (64.8%) (1999). The questionnaire approach used by Westat is far from adequate, but it helps agencies think about their services from the perspective of their outcomes on the community.

NSF-Funded Examination of Community Technology Centers

The "Impact of CTCNet Affiliates," a report issued in 1998, builds on a qualitative study of community technology centers done a year earlier (Chow et al. 1998). Of particular note is that this research was funded by the National Science Foundation, a departure for this agency that in the past had not seen the value of qualitative approaches to evaluation. The report

> describes results from a survey of 817 people, ages 13 to 91, at 44 community-based technology centers affiliated with the Community Technology Centers' Network (CTCNet). CTCNet affiliates include libraries, youth organizations, multiservice agencies, stand-alone computing centers, cable access centers, housing development centers, settlement houses, and various other non-profit organizations. Their common thread is that they all provide access to computers and related technologies, typically (but not entirely) to underserved or otherwise disadvantaged populations. Building on prior research conducted in 1997, this study was designed to increase understanding of the effect of community technology centers, particularly in the domains of employment, learning, personal gains, and sense of community (Chow et al. 1998).

The Community Connector (http://www.si.umich.edu/Community/) summarizes the findings: "The survey found that women and people of color make up the majority of centers' users (62% of respondents were female, 66% were non-white). Sixty-five percent of respondents took centers' classes to improve their job skills; 30% used the centers' Internet access to look for jobs. A majority of users said an important reason for coming to the center was learning about local events, local government, or state/federal government."[1]

In the report CTCNet researchers identify specific factors that affect people who use CTCs, many of whom come from disadvantaged populations. Areas of impact include employment, learning, personal gains, and a sense of community. Within these areas, specific effects were identified including the following:

work-related benefits such as improved job skills, improved computer skills

access to employment opportunities

education and improved outlook on learning

new skills and knowledge

personal efficacy and affective outcomes (general improvement in their life, their confidence, their outlook on life, and their future prospects; feelings of accomplishment and hope)

changes in the use of time and resources

increased civic participation

changes in social and community connections

technological literacy (i.e., improved perceptions of technology) as a means to achieve individual goals

more effective use of technology

appreciation for access to hardware, software, and video

general enjoyment and appreciation of the center

IMLS

Within the framework discussed previously, to prepare librarians for the changes that they will need to make in their approaches to evaluation, and to gain an ability to determine service benefits from the perspective of use,

IMLS issued a white paper in mid-2000 that challenges librarians and museum curators to rethink the way they currently evaluate public services. "The work of museums and libraries . . . takes place in an era of increasing demands for accountability. Such demands have already become a legislative reality with the passage of the Government Performance and Results Act (GPRA)" (2000).

The authors of this report caution that "in growing numbers, service providers, governments, other funders, and the public are calling for clearer evidence that the resources they expend actually produce benefits for people"(18). They point out that "if museums and libraries do not take the responsibility for developing their own set of credible indicators, they risk having someone else do it for them."

Examples at the State and Local Levels of Government

A number of state agencies and local governments have begun to develop outcome or performance tools that can be used to determine the extent to which taxpayers are getting their money's worth. *Maine's Guide to Performance Measurement* developed by the Maine Bureau of the Budget and the State Planning Office is one example of these efforts (1999). Its developers point out that this document is not unique; rather it was modeled on other current work, and its principal source was the Commonwealth of Virginia's Department of Planning and Budget's *Virginia's Planning and Performance Handbook* (1999). The *Maine Guide* is the result of legislation at the state level requiring new measures of accountability "for each of the state's budget programs to which it appropriates or allocates funds."

> A key goal of performance measurement is to assist decision-makers with fully assessing governmental performance. . . . Citizen skepticism of government performance can be allayed, in part, by a full and clear scrutiny of public performance. For this reason, the performance measurement system is not complete until results are reported externally to citizens and stakeholders. Only then can . . . citizens understand the value of state services for their tax dollars spent (*Maine's Guide to Performance Measurement* 1999).

The Multnomah County Auditor's report, *Service Efforts and Accomplishments Feasibility Study (SEA)*, issued in 2000, is an example of activity at the local level that builds on earlier work (Flynn 2000). This report notes that Multnomah County "has a strong history of performance measurement, evaluation, and benchmarking." The auditor sees this new approach as citizen-driven because "we cannot assume what is important or known by the public" (2000). In the process they learned from the public that citizens wanted reports "from the public's point of view" (2000).

Facing and Overcoming Evaluation Challenges

The challenge is to develop tools that will, on the one hand, effectively tell the story of what differences library CI services make and will, on the other hand, be used. Without appropriate tools for evaluating their initiatives in digital community services and community building, libraries may not be able to justify the receipt of public support and will experience difficulty in adapting their services to meet the growing needs of the public for information in new formats.

The tools librarians need can be built on the work we have done in this IMLS-sponsored study; they will identify indicators of impact that reflect the social context in which individuals access and use digital community services. These new tools will be context-based and should be easily implemented. They will need to capture richness and show patterns that reflect how digital community services affect people's lives. They will help librarians determine how digital community services help and will need to show how community organizations, citizens, and communities benefit from public library digital community services and how these services build community.

Such a suite of tools will be developed by our new study, "How Libraries and Librarians Help: Context-Centered Methods for Evaluating Public Library Efforts at Bridging the Digital Divide and Building Community." In the process we will: assess librarians' evaluation needs, tool requirements, and current practices; identify candidate impact indicators regarding individuals, non-profit organizations, and the larger community; develop tools that librarians can easily implement that will yield clear indicators; field test the usability and quality of these tools; make the tools easily accessible to public librarians; and use the power of Web technology to disseminate our tools and findings. Finally, to assure that such new and unfamiliar tools become accepted by opinion leaders, gate-keepers, and librarians, we will collaborate with organizations whose constituencies will benefit and develop evaluation training workshops.

REFERENCE

1. http://databases.si.umich.edu/cfdocs/community/rrdisplay.cfm?topic=Community+Technology+Centers/.

7

Learning from Best Practice

Summary, Conclusions, Recommendations

This book, based on the most extensive study ever conducted of how public libraries provide digital community information (CI), shows how public libraries and librarians harness the power of the Internet to increase access to information in their communities. We have provided a rich description of how public libraries participate in community networking activities. Our discussion of the benefits of bringing digital CI to American communities has revealed a gold mine of approaches showing how libraries and librarians help citizens get information for their daily lives. These CI activities have resulted in an increased ability to meet user information needs, viable partnerships with other community organizations, and a wide variety of individual and community benefits. The resulting gains have brought cachet to libraries and librarians through an increased understanding by citizens and community leaders of the value of public libraries in the community.

Underway: A Revolution in Community Information Provision

The Internet has made it possible for librarians to revolutionize the way they provide CI. Never before has CI been available twenty-four hours a day, seven days a week—not only to audiences across town but to people across the world. Librarians now bring CI to far broader audiences than they served with traditional CI services. While some libraries still hide their CI under the proverbial bushel basket (buried three, four, five, or six clicks from the top of the website or hidden within an obscure heading), increasingly librarians have taken advantage of the power of their library's website to give a considerably higher profile to CI.

CI has been transformed from a specialized information service to a highly visible, essential resource. Librarians have developed impressive examples of CI databases that easily interface with the Internet. They now bring a wide range of CI formats, including their digitized collections of local information and innovative applications such as geographic information systems (GIS). In the past if a library had CI, it was because staff had gone to great effort to collect it and store it. That approach has been greatly modified. No longer must a library own all its information.

For several years now many, if not most, local governments and community agencies have provided information about themselves on the Web. However, presence on the Web does not necessarily result in the linkages necessary for effective use of information about the community. Where effective linking across agencies does occur, it is most likely through a CN with strong public library involvement. Effectively networked CI results from a variety of proactive approaches including well-designed display of CI, outreach to agencies and non-profits, leadership in convincing agencies of the value of sharing information, and awareness and training activities. These approaches showcase librarians' leadership and skill in bringing together digital CI resources from a variety of agencies and organizing them for effective use.

The most important outcome of digital CI on the Web has unquestionably been increased use of CI. The Internet has made it possible for librarians to even capture an audience that may in the past have considered the library irrelevant to their needs. It has fostered use of local information by people who don't currently reside in the community but who need local information. Using the Internet to prominently display CI sends a strong message that the library plays a leadership role in providing relevant information for the community. When organizations see the value of working with the library CI, they do link to this valuable resource and encourage others to do the same. CI activities greatly increase the library's visibility, its partnerships, and its recognition in the community. Increased visibility has helped more citizens see librarians as trusted information professionals who are experts in increasing access to relevant CI resources—and who help them get the information they need. This heightened awareness continues to increase the number of people who see the local public library as a vital community agency.

Who Needs and Uses Community Information?

We gathered systematic evidence of citizens' online information behavior while searching for CI on the Internet. Through our case studies we examined the involvement in CNs of a number of community non-profit organizations. We investigated the role of librarians in providing digital CI as well as assistance in its use. Finally we examined and determined a range of impacts of library participation both in the provision of digital CI and as partners in community networking; and we identified digital CI best practices for emulation by other public libraries and communities.

The CN users in our study included men and women of all ages. They sought CI for personal and work-related situations with an emphasis on CI about employment, volunteerism, and social service availability, along with local history and genealogy, local news, computer and technical information, and other people (residing both within and beyond the community). Users' situations were complex and usually required multiple pieces and sources of CI, hence they often tried other sources (friends, newspapers, telephone directories, etc.) before turning to the network. In this sense, we learned that the Internet has not replaced the role of social ties in citizens' information behavior; instead, it is supplementing their information-seeking. One interesting example has been our finding that some users search for CI on behalf of another person (but not always at that person's behest).

People don't simply look for information. They want to use it. The Internet helps people search for other people online, sell and trade goods, research their family histories, exchange neighborhood information, and so on—all at a faster, more immediate pace. Increased access to the Internet, and hence CI, especially that which has been brought together by CNs and public libraries, has led to an increased public awareness of what's available, what's going on and what might be found in a community. Whereas people once relied on conversations over backyard fences, postings on notice boards at supermarkets, and local newspapers, they are now drawing upon the capabilities of the Internet to seek and share information about their communities. Public librarians are key players in increasing the flow of CI.

As we expected, people did encounter major barriers when seeking to use CI. The majority were information-related barriers encountered when using the Internet to get CI. People reported retrieving more information than they could digest; they encountered poor interface design, poorly organized information, dead links, information that was out of date, inaccurate, or missing. Likewise users found it difficult to gauge the quality of the CI source. Other barriers that prevented people from successfully obtaining CI pertained to technology and search skill levels, economics, geography, cognitive understanding, and psychological factors. Despite facing barriers our respondents indicated that they benefited from an increased ability to access CI, and they believe the CN helped them access hard-to-get and higher quality information more easily with decreased transaction costs (time and money). Thus it is clear that CNs provide access to CI that previously had been scattered and difficult to use.

Benefits of Community Information

What Differences Do Library Services Make in the Lives of Individuals?

The study that this book is based on examined the benefits from the perspective of their impact on citizens, community organizations, and the larger community. This is a radical departure from the way that libraries typically evaluate their services. We found many examples of librarians who had learned of ways that CI had made specific contributions to the lives of people and had contributed to making the neighborhood a better place to live in. To show the cumulative impact of anecdotal data, we grouped our data into representative categories of impact. People reported a number of personal benefits including: increased skill and confidence, employment and educational gains, increased knowledge of community, and benefits that accrued to their family, friends, and neighborhood. The personal assistance people received in seeking CI often empowered them to do something they had been unable to do previously. Both citizens and non-profit organizations report that their CN helped them overcome various barriers, including geographical, digital divide, and personal confidentiality concerns. Our data show indicators of increased social capital.

People reported successfully making connections with other people and groups. We found, in addition, that people seek and obtain assistance that results in neighborhood and community improvement.

The Quintessential Digital CI Payoff: Community Networking

As powerful as the direct benefits of CNs are, they do more than help the people who use them. They seem to have a multiplier effect that extends beyond the information obtained. They affect the community organizations that use them to reach out to their constituencies (such as the disabled or the homeless or those who serve parents or the unemployed). CNs build connections among community-serving organizations. Organization leaders actively involved with a CN reported that they had personally gained Internet knowledge and skills from participating. They, in turn, applied these new skills to their own organization. These leaders reported, in addition, that their organization's involvement in the CN resulted in an increased ability to be more responsive to their constituency and the community.

We found that CN involvement actually helped community organization leaders come to value such activities as information sharing, the effective organization of information, the importance of trusted sources of information, and the need to maintain current information. Likewise, we found that these organization leaders, as a result of thinking differently about information, began to consider themselves as information providers (IPs). Leaders who see their organizations as IPs are able to visualize how their organization (and its information) relates to the information and services of other groups. These impacts extend well beyond the effective use of information. They result in building a virtual framework for community. An important side-effect of this "multiplier" view is increased respect for the knowledge and skills that librarians bring to the community.

Common Approaches: Lessons Learned from Best Practice

How do library staff accomplish the feats that we have identified? Each CN reflects the mission of its parent organization and, just as importantly, the knowledge, skills, and values of librarians. First of all, it is important to note that all the CNs we looked at as well as the best practice CI providers identified in the study were led by a professional who values making connections in the community. This leader might be the library director or he or she may serve as the director of CI programs or have some other title, but without exception, this professional has an external focus. These leaders take a proactive approach to identifying CI providers. They do it formally through their jobs, they do it informally through Kiwanis or voluntary activities in the community. They are very much aware of their leadership in providing CI and use this position to bring a wide range of IPs together.

Leaders of best practice CNs are able to assess local situations and conditions and develop models that fit the needs and capabilities of the community. The actual CN model developed results from a variety of community and library circumstances and consists of a range of content development and service considerations. Leaders of the three case-study CNs and many other CNs recognize the need to provide training and technical assistance to community organizations and non-profit groups; how they do it varies.

Our best practice libraries value and engage in active collaboration with other organizations. They are likely to convene or otherwise bring community organizations together (through public meetings, electronic discussion lists, etc.). They find different ways to show community groups the value of developing relevant content and linking to related organizations. Likewise they foster communication among community organizations; communication leads to the creation of new partnerships among community groups. The CN is a mechanism for modeling activities that result in increased collaboration, volunteerism, training, and other benefits to the community.

Toward Evaluating the Use and Value of Digital Community Information

Through this study we found that effective delivery of digital CI yields a wide range of benefits to individuals, their families and friends, their neighborhoods, community organizations, the library itself, and the larger community. However, when we asked librarians about the effectiveness of current tools to provide data on CI benefits in their communities, they said that the tools in current use were grossly inadequate. But many of these librarians were able to remember a time recently when they had learned how someone or some group had made use of CI; they sent us scores of examples of such benefits. However, most don't formally capture this information. Thus we have identified a gap between what is needed and existing tools. In short, this study has been a vehicle for bringing together extremely valuable data that can be used to develop desperately needed tools designed to help librarians demonstrate the impact of public library CI services.

APPENDIX

A

Literature Review

In this appendix we review past developments and research studies that were pertinent to our project. It is organized in three sections: historical overview of CI and public libraries; historical overview of CNs; and recent trends in the networked CI literature.

Historical Overview of Community Information and Public Libraries

People require equitable and easy access to local resources that can help them deal with the myriad situations that arise through daily living, such as finding new jobs, childcare services, meal delivery or visiting nursing for aging parents, and state regulations for solving tenant disputes with landlords. In this sense, CI may be broadly defined as:

> any information that helps citizens with their day-to-day problems and enables them to fully participate as members of their community. It [includes] information pertaining to the availability of human services, such as health-care, financial assistance, housing, transportation, education, and child-care services; as well as information on recreation programs, clubs, community events, and information about all levels of government (Pettigrew 1996).

Public librarians have long recognized the importance of CI for creating and sustaining healthy communities. For almost three decades they have facilitated citizens' access to CI by providing information and referral (I&R) services, and, perhaps more importantly, through organizing and supporting community-wide information initiatives with local service providers (Baker & Ruey 1988, Childers 1984, Durrance 1984b, Pettigrew 1997a). Public library CI services arose in direct response to white flight to suburbia, the decay of the inner city, and the urban riots that occurred in the late 1960s. Researchers during this period found that "citizens are uninformed about public and private resources, facilities, rights, and programs and frustrated in their attempts to get information required for everyday problem solving" (Kochen & Donohue 1976).

Public library I&R services were aimed at connecting individuals with appropriate community resources that might assist in solving particular problems. While librarians identified, organized, and managed large files of data about their communities, they also became effective intermediaries (who engaged in active question negotiation), developed services designed to meet every-day information needs, experimented with emerging information technologies, embraced marketing concepts, and learned to collaborate effectively with other community agencies (Durrance & Schneider 1996). Helping clients overcome obstacles (advocacy) and ensuring that appropriate resources were obtained (follow-up) were also described as I&R activities; however, they largely failed to become incorporated into standard public library I&R practice (Childers 1984, Durrance 1984b). During this same period, the funding of many I&R initiatives by external agencies provided researchers with opportunities for studying ways that CI service delivery might inform or enrich the practice of public librarianship (including reference) as well as service evaluation; and signaled a growth in the knowledge of citizens' every-day information needs and seeking (Childers 1984, Dervin et al. 1976, Durrance 1984b, Harris & Dewdney 1994, Zweizig 1979).

Findings from this body of research on every-day information seeking indicate that all citizens despite their occupation, education, financial status, or social ties encounter situations for which they require CI and thus turn to varied formal and informal sources. Research shows that many people encounter great difficulties in recognizing and expressing their needs for such information and in navigating the local human services web (Agada 1999, Chatman 1985, 1990, 1996, 1999, Chen & Hernon 1982, Dervin et al. 1976, Durrance 1984a, Harris 1988, Harris & Dewdney 1994, Palmour et al. 1979, Pettigrew 1997b, Savolainen 1995, Warner et al. 1973, Wilson 1997). Financial, physical, and geographic barriers also prohibit citizens from successfully seeking CI (Childers 1975). As a result, many citizens cannot obtain needed services and cannot participate in their community's democratic processes. According to a recent report from the National Telecommunications and Information Administration:

Significant segments of the population still remain unconnected by telephone and/or computer. [There] are still pockets of "have nots" among the low-income, minorities, and the young, particularly in rural areas and central cities. . . . These populations are among those, for example, that could most use electronic services to find jobs, housing, or other services. Because it may take time before these groups become connected at home, it is still essential that schools, libraries, and other community access centers provide computer access in order to connect significant portions of our population (McConnaughey & Lader 1998).

Substantial literature suggests that citizens prefer face-to-face communication when seeking help for every-day problems, and that institutional resources—including libraries—are often consulted as a last resort (cf, Harris & Dewdney 1994). For these reasons it is important to note that libraries exist as only one among many distinct access points through which individuals might obtain CI. Moreover, different communities follow different models including ones where libraries play supporting roles as CI managers that collect and channel CI to other service providers that the public might call upon for assistance.

Networked Community Information Systems

Recent initiatives of the National Telecommunications and Information Administration (1999), the Bill and Melinda Gates Foundation (1999), and the W. K. Kellogg Foundation (1999) aim at ensuring full connectivity in all of America's public libraries. While the purpose of these initiatives is to promote viable communities through equitable computer and Internet access, a result is greater collaboration among libraries, service providers, and other groups for improving public access to information about local resources. One such collaboration in which librarians have participated since the 1980s and is proliferating world-wide is community networking. These electronic consortia provide citizens with Internet access to CI and facilitate communication with other people through email, community-oriented discussions, and question-and-answer forums (Cisler 1996, Durrance 1993, 1994, 1997, Durrance & Schneider 1996, Schuler 1994, 1996). With an emphasis on community-building aspects, in its inaugural publication the Association for Community Networking defined community networking as occurring "when people and organizations collaborate locally to solve problems and create opportunities, supported by appropriate information and communication systems." They define a CN as a "locally-based, locally-driven communication and information system" (Gonzalez 1998).

CI is often a central CN feature that appears in many forms: I&R agencies and libraries, for example, may mount their databases on the Internet, while individual service providers may post information about their programs and services. Thus the architecture of the Internet makes networked CI possible by linking information files created not only by single organizations such as libraries, but also by agencies, organizations, and individuals throughout the community (and, of course, the world). This is a major departure from traditional I&R services where librarians and other CI agency staff work with files about the community that are created on an internal library system.

Library participation in community networking is a particularly important partnership. While participation holds significant potential for improving citizens' access to CI, and hence, needed resources, it also requires substantial resource and staffing commitments of the public library along with serious consideration of its service mission. The implications for library participation in Internet-access initiatives were discussed recently by McClure and Bertot (1998), who remarked:

> Libraries' use of the Web significantly increases the range and extent of resources and services available to the residents of Pennsylvania and results in numerous benefits. These benefits, however, do not come without a price. The site visits found that the Web presence for many of these (and other libraries in the state) resulted from individually dedicated librarians and community volunteers who contributed significant time and effort to developing and maintaining the Website. The study found that many librarians wonder where the funding for maintenance and for the continuous upgrading of web-based service that the public demands will come from. Further, many libraries, particularly small libraries and branches are overwhelmed by the tremendous demand for such services (25).

But as a result of community networking and the Internet, citizens can access networked CI through terminals in their public library while seeking help with related search problems from librarians. In short, networked CI means that citizens can access CI at any time and from any place, including the home, office, and public library.

Life in an electronic world poses several fundamental problems for research by the library and information science community. Two such questions that are just beginning to be addressed include:

How do citizens seek help using networked CI?

How are public libraries facilitating citizens' CI needs by participating in networked CI initiatives such as community networking?

These questions reflect those succinctly articulated by Savolainen (1999) and Bishop (1997). In her course syllabus at the University of Illinois, Bishop raises important questions about CNs such as:

the degree to which they strengthen social bonds as opposed to weakening them by reducing face-to-face interactions;

the extent to which they are used by people representing the full socioeconomic spectrum;

the degree to which their use helps solve community problems;

their ability to maintain valuable and accurate online CI resources;

the extent to which they present people with usable interfaces and information retrieval mechanisms; and

the degree to which they are sustainable as organizations.

Schement also impressed the importance of understanding the context in which citizens seek information and adopt new technologies (Benton Foundation and Libraries for the Future 1997). In reference to citizens in the information and technology age, he observed that while "the real transition is local, its implications are global," and forewarned that libraries "lag in [their] understanding of the social context—a context in which libraries will have to justify themselves." He suggested libraries should consider "how Americans [will] live their lives as citizens, as economic actors, and as social beings" in the coming decades. Putnam (1995, 2000) made similar observations in reference to the decline of social capital in American communities.

Research Trends in the Networked CI Literature

The mixed potential of the Internet for promoting library growth was discussed as early as 1993 by public library leaders and managers, who suggested that "real, down-to-earth" information services and products would be necessary "if John Q. Public was to use [the] public library to access the Internet" (McClure, Ryan, & Moen 1993). They suggested that libraries provide public Internet access to "community-based information services in health care, community activities, and unique local resources; Job-net; government databases; and practical electronic discussion lists such as auto repair" (26–27), and that libraries participate in community networking initiatives (at the time referred to as free-nets). But what has happened since 1993? Have public libraries started offering services and products that address the public's every-day information needs? If so, how is the public using networked CI services, specifically?

According to Bertot and McClure's (1998a) systematic study of public library connectivity, 83.6% of U.S. public libraries are connected to the Internet in some way, and 87.7% of those connected also offer public access. However, questions remain regarding the types of networked CI services libraries offer and how the public uses these services. To date, comprehensive data regarding public library participation and citizen use of networked CI services are unavailable. Little is known, for example, about how many and what types of libraries are involved in community networking initiatives and what this involvement entails with regard to such organizational concerns as funding, staffing, and programming. In-depth examinations are also lacking regarding citizens' information behavior in networked CI environments, such as the types of situations that prompt citizens to seek CI online, how the information helps, and the role of intermediaries such as reference librarians. Other imminent questions concern the community-wide impact of networked CI provision and whether such initiatives foster effective community building and social capital. If a primary purpose of networked CI services is to strengthen communities by facilitating the public's needs for information through inter-agency cooperation, then these questions (among others) must be addressed. Answers will assist practitioners in deciding whether and how to offer networked CI services, and will contribute to general knowledge of citizens' information behavior.

Across the spectrum, academics, professionals, service providers, government, and funding agencies agree that both basic research and empirical evaluation of existing networked CI services are needed. However, as a review of the literature reveals, only small pockets of systematic research are underway, and this body of work is spread across different countries and is sometimes incorporated as a subsection of a larger report on a related topic such as connectivity (e.g., the McClure & Bertot studies). In general, the literature can be divided among three categories: papers that focus *primarily* (albeit some overlap does occur and thus categories are not entirely mutually exclusive) on networked CI services through (1) public libraries, (2) CNs, and (3) other service providers that make information about their services available on-line. Papers focusing on networked CI may be then sub-classified along five lines:

1. *Basic research*—the authors discuss results from an empirical study of, for example, networked CI design or users' information needs, seeking, or use that is grounded in a conceptual framework and is aimed at making contributions to a particular area of knowledge.

2. *Policy research*—the authors assess the impact of federal, state, or local government policy regarding such issues as universal service and public access on public library ability to provide networked CI services.

3. *Applied research*—the authors discuss results from an empirical study of, for example, networked CI design, or users' information needs, seeking, or use, where the primary aim is to produce results that can be applied in a particular empirical context.

4. *Argumentation*—the authors discuss reasons for service provider (including public library) participation in networked CI provision, and so on.

5. *Descriptive*—with respect to a particular organization or network the authors describe how networked CI services were implemented, discuss policy such as acceptable use or posting standards, or focus on technological aspects such as interface design, telecommunications, or hardware/software requirements in networked CI provision.

Table A.1 shows a matrix formed by listing these three major categories and five sub-categories for types of papers. Each cell contains the authors and publication year of representative papers. Schuler's works from 1994 and 1996, for example, are grouped under "community networks—descriptive" because he describes different CNs in terms of their organization, requirements, services, and so on. In a similar vein, Bluming and Mittleman (1996) discuss benefits of the Los Angeles Free-Net for health information users. Milio (1996), on the other hand, addresses the need for electronic health networks to include CI, while Borgstrom (1998) argues that CNs should seek external funding and nurture outside contacts more aggressively, and Howley (1998) explains the significance of human computer interaction for networked CI provision. Thus, these three papers are grouped under "community networks—argumentation."

TABLE A.1   Networked Community Information Literature—Paper Types

NCI Focus / Type of Paper	Public Libraries	Community Networks	Service Providers/ Government
Basic Research	McClure/Bertot (1997, 1998)	*Avis (1995) Bertot/McClure (1996) Bishop (submitted) Bishop et al. (in press) Cohill/Kavanaugh (1997) *Guy (1996) *Morgan (1997) Pettigrew/Wilkinson (1996) *Roberts (1996) Toms/Kinnucan (1996) Vaughan/Schwartz (1999)	Savolainen (in press)
Policy Research	Bertot/McClure (1997) Bertot/McClure (1998a&b) McClure et al (1993) Ormes/McClure (1997)		
Applied Research	Elliott (1995) Geffert (1993) Harvey/Horne (1995) Jokitalo (1997) Knox/Durrance (1997) Mattison (1994) Morson et al. (1996) Newton et al. (1998) Resnick (1997)	*Beamish (1995) Chow et al. (1998) Clark (1997) Harsh (1995) Patrick (1996, 1997) Patrick/Black (1996a&b) Patrick et al. (1995) *Ryan (1996) Schalken/Tops (1994) **Surak (1998) *Thompson (1997) Yerkey (1997)	Guard et al. (1997) Hallam/Murray (1998) Rathbone (1997) Wyman et al. (1997)

NCI *Focus* *Type of Paper*	*Public* *Libraries*	*Community* *Networks*	*Service Providers/* *Government*

Argumentation	Batt (1996)
	Durrance/
	  Schneider
	  (1996)
	Pratt (1997)
	Schuler (1997)
		Borgstrom (1998)
		Durrance (1997)
		Howley (1998)
		Milio (1996)
			Pettigrew/
			Wilkinson (1994)

Descriptive	Berkowitz/Brodie
	  (1996)
	Fietzer (1996)
	Fox (1995)
	Gall/Miller (1997)
	Gallimore (1997)
	Hale (1996)
	Hubbard et al.
	  (1996)
	Mansfield (1997)
	McLeod (1997)
	Stearns (1996)
	Welling (1996)
	Wening (1997)
		Archee (1995)
		Bluming/Mittelman
		  (1996)
		Fichter/Martin
		  (1997a&b)
		Guard (1996)
		Maciuszko (1990)
		Newby/Bishop
		  (1996)
		Schuler (1994, 1996)
		Woods (1996)
			Stapleton (1997)

Note: Cells contain authors' names and publication year of representative papers.

* MA Thesis   ** Honors Thesis

Although the matrix is not inclusive of all papers published on networked CI provision, the distribution nonetheless suggests that the vast majority of papers, whether they focus primarily on public libraries or CNs, are of an applied or descriptive nature. Also of interest is that four of the nine papers considered "community network—basic research" were masters' theses. The overall richness of the papers examined suggests that several research directions are emerging that warrant systematic investigation. As shown in table A.2, the forty-six research papers (applied, basic, and policy) encompass varied aspects of networked CI services, including community development, evaluation of public library initiatives, government CI, history and organization, human-computer interaction, human information behavior (i.e., how individuals need, seek, and use networked CI), policy (e.g., federal, state, or local government; and information control and ownership), public library connectivity, training, and the voluntary sector.

**TABLE A.2   Networked Community Information Literature—
Research Paper Topics**

Topic	Examples
Community Development	Avis (1995), Guard et al. (1997), Guy (1996), Morgan (1997), Roberts (1996)
Evaluation (public library networked information services)	Bertot/McClure (1996), Geffert (1993), Knox/Durrance (1997), Mattison (1994), McClure/Bertot (1997), McClure et al. (1993), Resnick (1997)
Government CI	Wyman et al. (1997)
History and Organization	Beamish (1995), Ryan (1996), Surak (1998)
Human-Computer Interaction	Toms/Kinnucan (1996), Vaughan/Schwartz (1999)
Human Information Behavior	Bishop (submitted), Bishop et al. (in press), Chow (1998), Clark (1997), Cohill/Kavanaugh (1997), Elliott (1995), Harsh (1995), Harvey/Horne (1995), Jokitalo (1997), McClure/Bertot (1998), Morson et al. (1996), Patrick (1996, 1997), Patrick/Black (1996a&b), Patrick et al. (1995), Savolainen (in press), Schalken/Tops (1994)
Policy	Bertot/McClure (1997), Pettigrew/Wilkinson (1996)
Public Library Connectivity	Bertot/McClure (1998a&b), Newton et al. (1998), Ormes/McClure (1997)
Training	Yerkey (1997)
Transportation CI	Rathbone (1997)
Voluntary Sector	Hallam/Murray (1998), Thompson (1997)

Several authors, including those of descriptive papers, discussed networked CI services with regard to specific types of information such as health (Bluming & Mittelman 1996, Clark 1997, Fichter & Martin-Brownell 1997a, Guard et al. 1996, Milio 1996), transportation (Rathbone 1997), or particular geographic areas (Guy 1966). Others focused on cross-cultural comparisons (e.g., Ormes & McClure 1997, Surak 1998) and interagency cooperation (e.g., Fichter & Martin-Brownell 1997b, Gall & Miller 1997, Pettigrew & Wilkinson 1994, Schuler 1997). Although questionnaires remain a popular form of data collection, multiple qualitative and quantitative methods were used, especially by authors whose papers were grouped under "basic research."

The conceptual frameworks authors employed were as varied, as one might expect, as the research topics therein. Toms and Kinnucan (1996), for example, used theoretical models of metaphor and visual representation in interface design, while Bertot and McClure (1997) developed a national data collection paradigm for evaluating public library Internet connectivity that they have used in several studies. Bishop, Tidline, Shoemaker, and Salela (1999) studied users' information behavior from an information poverty perspective, while Pettigrew and Wilkinson (1996) used an information access policy framework, and Savolainen (in press) and Morgan (1997) drew upon "way of life" and community attachment theory, respectively.

In answer to the questions "Have public libraries started offering services and products that address the public's every-day information needs? And, if so, how is the public using networked CI services?" there is little doubt that libraries *are* participating in networked CI provision in varied ways. However, systematic research on the types and degree of service provision is lacking: the evidence to date only confirms that the phenomenon is occurring. While self- and anecdotal reports, along with the results from large, general studies conducted by McClure and Bertot (with others), the Council on Library Resources (1996), and the Benton Foundation & Libraries for the Future (1997) as well as from small-scale investigations (e.g., Resnick 1997), for example, indicate that public libraries are involved in networked CI provision (frequently through community networking), comprehensive data regarding indicators of nationwide participation and organizational impact are currently unavailable.

Correspondingly, there exists a paucity of solid evidence regarding citizens' information behavior when interacting with networked CI, specifically on the situations that prompt users to seek networked CI, their perceptions while seeking and interacting with networked CI providers and systems, and the uses that individuals make of the information, that is, how the CI helps (cf, Dervin & Nilan 1986). Instead, and consistent with Julien's (1996) observations of the general needs-and-uses literature published from 1990-1994, most related networked CI studies are from the professional literature and report user and use statistics. Thus it seems that the early networked CI literature is akin to the general public literature that Zweizig and Dervin (1977) criticized as providing little insight into the uses that people make of information and information systems. Moreover, the findings from these studies often conflict, especially with regard to user socio-demographics. In short, while respondents, such as those in Geffert's survey (1993), indicate that they value public access to networked CI in libraries, systematic research is sorely needed.

The more encouraging note—as witnessed by the eighteen papers grouped under human information behavior—is that research interest in citizens' use of networked CI is increasing. Savolainen, in his typology of empirical research on networked information use, concluded that "use studies in the context of non-work activities still form a minority but interests towards this sub field seem to be growing." In remarking on the rising popularity of triangulated qualitative research methods, he added that such studies might be rendered "more profound" by employing "approaches [that] discuss the use of networked services as part of everyday life practices" (1998, 342). On the whole, Savolainen's observations are equally tenable in this review: while a majority of the applied and descriptive studies employ questionnaires or analyze transaction log data that reveal user socio-demographics and system or page use frequency (e.g., Harsh 1995, Harvey & Horne 1995, Patrick 1996, 1997, Patrick & Black 1996a&b, Patrick et al. 1995, Schalken & Tops 1994), there is a definite movement towards using multiple qualitative methods (e.g., in-depth interviewing, structured observation, participant diary-keeping, focus groups, etc.) in conjunction with quantitative approaches.

Three studies of particular note are Bishop et al. (1999) and McClure and Bertot (1997, 1998), which used multiple methods to investigate the types of information that citizens seek online and its uses. Rich findings were reported by Bishop et al. regarding household interviews and focus groups in low-income neighborhoods with users and potential users of the Prairienet CN. The most frequently cited CI need concerned "health, parenting, education, leisure activities, and employment opportunities." As Bishop et al. further reported:

Interview respondents also wanted more easily accessible information about available and affordable services of all kinds . . . services provided by organizations like the Urban League or Salvation Army, and those relating to rent subsidy and food banks were frequently mentioned. In addition to subsistence information, participants . . . sought information about church, sports and recreational activities, local government, creative pursuits, legal services, and volunteer opportunities.

Responses regarding needs for networked CI were similar. Bishop et al. identified the following areas (in order of frequency): community services and activities, resources for children, healthcare, education, employment, crime and safety, and general reference tools. When seeking CI respondents identified personal contacts at community organizations and close members of their social networks as the most important sources, which were valued for their "advice" and "recommendations." For obtaining networked CI, respondents "consistently recommended public libraries, community and public housing recreation centers, and social service organizations as public access computing sites." In discussing the advantages and drawbacks of both home and public CN access, Bishop et al. remarked that "computer use will not readily take hold among low-income community residents until they are able to find a way around the splintered ecology of access within which they currently live." Their recommendations for how libraries might provide more effective networked information services are aimed at complementing citizens' lifestyles, constraints, and information seeking patterns.

Two other major studies that examined citizens' needs for networked CI were conducted by McClure and Bertot (1997, 1998), who focused on Pennsylvania public library use. From desk log anecdotes, they identified several types of library impact, including: impacts of critical information, local history and genealogy benefits, educational benefits, economic benefits, medical and legal impacts, technological impacts, benefits from pleasant environment, socialization and networking impacts, and impacts on the hard-to-serve. Similar to Bishop et al., the 1998 findings reported by McClure and Bertot are very rich, especially with regard to the specific types of situations that prompt citizens to seek CI—including networked CI—at libraries. Of the many concrete examples they offer, one includes a patron who was a victim of a physical attack and needed legal information (beyond that provided by the authorities) about her rights. A second example involves a patron who works with welfare recipients who are about to lose their benefits. A third situation shows a patron who needed information about admitting someone to a long-term care facility. As one respondent explained, "the library is a resource for the community to use to solve its most difficult problems and to resolve life's worst troubles" (26). With regard to Internet use (1997), in particular, it was public access that drew 26% of survey respondents to the library (N=1,925). Moreover, 34.5% of respondents had no other form of Internet access, and while the majority reported positive experiences with system use they comprised both experienced and novice users.

In sum, it appears that public libraries have begun offering networked CI services as part of renewed efforts at meeting the needs of John and Jane Q. Public, and that citizens do access this CI through library terminals and from other venues. However, as our review of the literature indicates, only a few researchers have begun to address the situational or contextual factors that prompt citizens to seek CI online, how networked CI helps (or does not help) citizens with daily living, and how it affects their overall help-seeking or information behavior, especially with regard to public libraries. Moreover, little research has focused specifically on the national impact of networked CI provision on public libraries, the degree to which public libraries are participating in community networking, the role of reference service in networked CI provision, and on how public libraries and their service provider partners expect networked CI will help their clients and communities. Without appropriate tools for evaluating their participation in networked CI provision and community networking specifically, libraries cannot entirely justify the receipt of public support and cannot fully adapt their services to meet the growing needs of the public for information in new formats. Tools designed in the 1980s and 1990s (e.g., Kindel 1995, Robbins & Zweizig 1988, Zweizig et al. 1994) are not entirely adequate for evaluating electronic service delivery since they do not account—in Bertot and McClure's (1997) terms—for the complex multi-dimensionality of electronic networks. As a result, planners are encountering difficulties with measuring the impact of networked CI services on users, communities, and libraries (as organizations), and therefore cannot determine whether such Internet initiatives are effective and cost-efficient in terms of resource and staff allocation.

Answers to the questions posed earlier remain elusive. While it is evident that public libraries are offering public Internet access and that they are participating in community networking initiatives, researchers have just begun to explore citizens' seeking and use of networked CI.

B

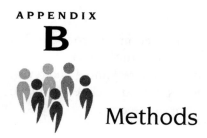

Methods

Our large-scale investigation of CI and public libraries
was unprecedented and attempted to address major gaps
in the professional and research literatures. In this appendix we describe
the different methods that we used to address our project's objectives and
research questions, along with the measures we implemented to ensure the
validity and reliability of our data.

The study comprised two major phases: (1) a two-stage, nation-wide
survey with public library directors and CI staff, and (2) intensive case
studies using multiple data collection methods of public library–community networking systems in three communities.

PHASE ONE
Public Library Surveys

To gather baseline data regarding the extent and nature of public library
involvement in CI provision, we sent a brief survey to a stratified, random
sample of the directors of 725 medium and large-size libraries. An overwhelming 69.66% (N=505) of directors responded to that survey. This
was followed by a second survey, which was sent to 227 CI coordinators,
whose names were provided by the library directors that participated in
the first survey. This second survey comprised a sixteen-page, seventy-four
question instrument that focused in detail on all aspects of CI provision in
1999. The response rate for survey 2 was 59.91% (N=136). The initial
sample was drawn using the U.S. Department of Education's Federal State
Cooperative System and with the assistance of Keith Lance (consultant),
Director of the Colorado Library Research Service. We employed a two-stage approach for the survey because we had no other way of identifying

which staff at which libraries were heavily involved in CI provision. No data were available at any agency that could assist with this identification. The results from these surveys are discussed in chapters 3 and 4 and reveal rich, unprecedented findings regarding the extent and scope of public library involvement in CI provision at the turn of the century.

PHASE TWO
Case Studies

For the main part of our study we conducted intensive case studies using triangulated methods in three communities (in three states) that have been nationally recognized for their respective CN and in which the local public library system plays a leading role. These systems, NorthStarNet (IL), the Three Rivers Free-Net (PA), and CascadeLink (OR), are described in terms of their locales, areas served, affiliated library system, and establishment year in table B.1.

In any qualitative study, the primary data collection instrument is the researcher; yet it is also standard to use multiple methods of data collection (triangulation) to increase the trustworthiness of the data. For this reason, at each field study site we used a standard template or design that

TABLE B.1   Overview of Data Collection Sites

Site	Counties/Areas Served	Public Library System	Community Network	
			Name	*Date Established*
Northeastern Illinois	Cook, DuPage, Kane, Lake, McHenry, and Will	Suburban Library System	NorthStarNet (nsn.nslsilus.org)	1995
Pittsburgh, Pennsylvania	Southwestern Pennsylvania	Carnegie Library of Pittsburgh	Three Rivers Free-Net (trfn.clpgh.org)	1995
Portland, Oregon	Multnomah County	Multnomah County Library	CascadeLink (www.cascade link.org)	1996

comprised an online survey and follow-up telephone interviews with selected adult CN users who accessed tagged CI web pages; and in-depth interviews,[1] field observation,[2] and focus groups with public library–CN staff, local human service providers, and members of the public, along with extensive note-keeping by members of our research team, which included the principal investigators and graduate student assistants. To facilitate our data collection, we used separate guides for our interviews with different types of participants.[3] For this reason, we used several methods of data collection. All data collection instruments were pre-tested and approved by the Human Subjects Divisions in the Offices for Research at the University of Michigan and the University of Washington. Informed consent was sought from all participants. A letter of information and a consent form was designed for the users, library staff and service providers. Strict confidentiality was assured for all participants, which was maintained by assigning unique codes to the library–CNs, library sites, agencies, and service providers that were part of the study or were identified by participants during data collection. All personal identifiers were removed from data collection forms and transcripts.

User Online Survey and Follow-up Interviews

The purpose of the online survey was to gather baseline data regarding user socio-demographics and online CI use, including from where users access the network (e.g., from home, work, library terminals). Using the sense-making approach, the survey included questions regarding the reasons the user accessed CI pages, how the user intended to use the CI, what type of help he or she expected to receive, and what kinds of barriers he or she encountered in seeking help for the situation. Since previous research indicates that some users primarily use CNs to communicate with other members, the online survey appeared only to those who accessed a page that contained CI. In brief, the first time a user accessed a tagged page (all top-level CI pages were tagged), a link appeared that asked the user to click on the survey before logging off so he or she could complete it. The survey was posted, during different time periods, on each network. At the end of the survey, respondents were asked to participate in a thirty-minute telephone interview about their use of the Internet. Interviews with selected respondents were held at times that were convenient for them.

The purpose of these follow-up interviews was to gain in-depth insights regarding their use of the library and the Internet for obtaining CI electronically. The micro-moment, timeline interview method was used to collect these data. The number of days each survey ran and the total number of responses for each network are summarized in table B.2.

In aggregate, 197 users responded to the online survey. The majority of respondents were from the Three Rivers Free-Net, which averaged 1.37 surveys per day posted. At both NorthStarNet and CascadeLink the average number of surveys received per day was 0.57. In-depth, follow-up interviews were conducted by telephone with twenty-seven online survey respondents. We were extremely satisfied with the response rate and concluded, from the clarity and richness of respondents' answers and comments, that respondents largely understood and were able to answer the survey's questions. The respondents' age groups followed a normal distribution with most respondents (71.4%) falling between the ages of 25 and 55, while slightly more women (54.6%) responded than men. Thus our findings suggest that a typical user is non-existent, socio-demographically

TABLE B.2   Overview of Online Survey Responses

Community Network/ Area Served	Number of Days Survey Posted	Number of Responses	Gender			Age Range						
			M	F	NA	18–25	25–35	36–45	46–55	56–65	66+	NA
NorthStarNet Northeastern Illinois	60	34	10	20	4	6	9	9	5	2	1	2
Three Rivers Free-Net Pittsburgh, Pennsylvania	90	123	57	61	5	10	30	22	30	15	9	7
CascadeLink Multnomah, County, Portland, Oregon	70	40	17	20	3	5	7	9	11	3	2	3
TOTAL	220	197	84	101	12	21	46	40	46	20	12	12

speaking: users equally represent both genders, a distributed range of age groups, and a diverse range of occupations from students to blue-collar workers to white-collar professionals. Our respondents also comprised both first-time or novice users as well as very experienced searchers.

On a conceptual level, both the online survey and follow-up interviews with selected respondents were based on Dervin's sense-making theory (cf, Dervin 1992, Savolainen 1993), which comprises a set of user-centered assumptions and methods for studying the uses individuals make of information systems. It asserts that throughout daily life, people encounter gaps in their knowledge that they can only bridge by making new sense of their situations. Thus they use varied strategies to seek and construct information from different resources or ideas as they cope with different barriers. Sense-making facilitates the study of different aspects of information behavior. Our research included two aspects: users' assessments of the helpfulness of digital CI, and users' and service providers' constructions or images of these systems. Both were investigated using the micro-moment timeline technique where respondents were asked "to reconstruct a situation in terms of what happened (timeline steps) [and then] to describe each step in detail" (70), which enabled us to gather and compare the perceptions of different players regarding how CI is constructed and used through electronic communication. The framework's social constructionist orientation suggested it would be viable for studying citizens' online information behavior.

Service Provider Interviews and Focus Groups

In addition to the online survey and follow-up interviews with CN users, we conducted in-depth interviews and focus groups with service providers whose websites or CI pages were accessed by the users we surveyed. These service providers were asked such questions as how they believe electronic access to their information helps clients, why they present CI in particular ways, how their organizations benefit from participating in the CN, what barriers they encounter, and so on. Their perceptions and expectations were analyzed in context of user's responses regarding the same, and for best practices among service providers. Examples of service providers who participated in the interviews and focus groups included policemen, municipal planners, and staff from local social service agencies.

Library Staff Observation,
Interviews, and Focus Groups

During our site visits, which ranged from three to five days, we also conducted field observation and focus groups (FGs) with library administrators, librarians, and other CN staff whose work included facilitating citizen's access to electronic CI. Through observation at different times of the week and day, we collected contextual, environmental data about real-time incidents in which librarians assisted users with Internet searches for CI, and we were able to discuss generic incidents with the librarians. During the focus groups we gathered librarian's perceptions of how their work, specifically, the reference interview, has been affected by providing CI Internet access. Librarians were questioned about how users present initial questions that result in accessing CI online, the kinds of questions users ask and the kinds of help users require when performing Internet searches for CI, how they believe this service helps clients, and how techniques such as meta-tagging facilitate citizen's searches. Data also were collected regarding best practices through both the observation and focus groups. In our interviews with library administrators and staff who participate in community networking we gained insights into their administrative concerns regarding library participation in community working and its impact on their organization and the community at-large.

The number of interviews and focus groups we conducted at each site with service providers and library staff are summarized in table B.3. Our

TABLE B.3   Number of Interviews and Focus Groups (FG)
by Data Collection Site

Group	Three Rivers Free-Net	NorthStarNet	CascadeLink
Service Providers	12 interviews	4 FGs with 19 participants	3 interviews + 1 FG with 8 participants
Library/CN Staff	5 interviews + 1 FG with 5 participants	7 interviews + 1 FG with 6 participants	8 interviews
Library Administrators	3 interviews	3 interviews + 1 FG with 5 participants	3 interviews

decision to audio-record the interviews and focus groups was largely based on the advantage the recorder offers of allowing the researchers to pay complete attention to the discussion (Lofland & Lofland 1995). Furthermore, participants were more likely to talk freely when being recorded than when not because in the latter case they may have been distracted by note taking. Thus using a recorder was a means of enhancing the quality of the data.

In summary, our investigation yielded the following types of field records in addition to the data obtained through our two-stage survey with public libraries:

Online survey with CN users transcripts

User interview informed consent form (verbal)

User interview field notes

User interview transcripts

Entry diaries for recording initial contacts and site visit scheduling

Preliminary site visit field notes

General site notes regarding library layout location

Library observation field notes

Library staff informed consent forms

Library staff interview/focus group audio-recordings

Library staff interview/focus group transcripts

Library staff interview/focus group field notes

Service provider informed consent forms

Service provider interview/focus group audio-recordings

Service provider interview/focus group transcripts

Service provider interview/focus group field notes

Miscellaneous (e.g., documents obtained at the libraries)

Methodological Issues
with Collecting Data Online

For researchers, the Internet represents a powerful mechanism for gathering data about the public and the use of different digital systems (Witte et al. 2000). But as Zhang (2000) points out, little research has been conducted on the validity and reliability of Internet methods, especially online surveys. She raises questions regarding: the conditions under which Internet surveys can be effective, what factors affect validity, how the implementation of some techniques may improve response rate and data quality, and how respondents react to Internet-based surveys during a survey session (57). Summarizing a multi-disciplinary literature, Zhang lists the following advantages of Internet-based surveys over conventional mail surveys:

research costs for sending questionnaires and coding data are lower;

turnaround times are shorter;

potential respondents are readily reached in geographically remote areas;

for research involving sensitive topics, particular populations such as drug dealers, gay and lesbian students, etc., may be reached more easily;

larger numbers of individuals may be surveyed more efficiently;

respondents may be more motivated to participate by the dynamic interactive nature of web-based surveys; and

errors may be reduced in data transcription and coding (58).

For our study, we chose to conduct online surveys because CN users were our population of interest, and hence posting our survey on the networks' CI pages seemed the best and most logical means of identifying and reaching potential respondents. Moreover, asking respondents to participate while they were in the process of actively seeking information online was consistent with the critical incident/timeline approach of our study's theoretical framework. In other words, we anticipated high reliability of users' responses if they completed the survey during an actual, real-time search since memory recall would not be problematic. However, we faced many challenges with using the Web to conduct our survey. The main difficulties included:

estimating the sample size from a population that was also unknown in size;

knowing that the sample would not be random or representative socio-demographically due to the self-selection of respondents;

the inability (and hence effect on validity) to clarify any questions of the respondents regarding the survey instrument;

how to pretest the instrument, given that we did not know how, sequentially, the respondents would participate in the survey (i.e., at the beginning of their search, midway, upon completion, etc.), which was complicated by the nature of hyperlinks;

creating an instrument that would be sufficiently short to encourage completion and yet in-depth enough to capture the data of theoretical interest;

creating an attractive layout, based on good design principles, that would encourage completion and yet followed the standards of the CN (some networks had restrictions regarding flashing banners, etc.);

determining where to post the survey (i.e., which pages—homepage only, CI main page only, specific CI pages, etc.);

selecting a database program for storing and managing responses that worked well with the CN software, and resolving technical bugs; and,

estimating the completion time-frame of the survey stage for project management purposes (had no basis for estimating response rate through time).

These factors build on those noted by Witte et al. (2000) and Zhang (2000), whose lists of potential concerns when conducting Internet-based surveys included: (1) the exclusion of some population segments due to lack of Internet access; (2) the discomfort that some individuals feel toward Internet formats and their perceptions of it being questionable or untrustworthy; (3) the high degree of respondent self-selection and its potential to introduce bias within a sample; (4) the validity of respondents (i.e., surveys can reach unintended individuals who cannot be screened); (5) multiple responses from the same respondent; (6) variation and difficulty in determining response rate; (7) the impersonalized nature of survey requests; and (8) the high level of expertise required of survey researchers, especially since respondents tend to "drop-out" before completing the survey or do not provide answers to some questions. Except for (1) (because we specifically targeted Internet users), all of these concerns factored in our study. Additionally, we were concerned about a possible Hawthorne effect where users might give responses because they felt positively towards the CN and wished to indicate their support.

Data Analysis

In keeping with our qualitative approach, we analyzed data as they were collected and followed an analytic approach recommended by Lofland

and Lofland (1995) and Miles and Huberman (1994), which consisted of coding, memoing, and diagramming. As a result, data collection and analysis became an iterative process in which each round of analysis guided the purposive collection of more data, and each return from the field led closer to an understanding of the phenomenon under study.

We coded the data using Glaser and Strauss's constant comparative method as the theoretical approach in which the coding of data is combined with the generation of theoretical ideas (1967). This is consistent with Strauss's "coding from the data" method (1987). The resulting schemes reflected the data's emergent themes and were guided by the study's conceptual framework. The following codebooks were developed:

> Users
>
> Service providers
>
> Public library staff

Using these codebooks, we assigned terms to all segments in the ethnographic records that reflected particular concepts. During the latter stages the collapsing of codes, such as types of CI, was based on theoretically derived categories and findings from the research literature and was always considered in terms of how the participants perceived the phenomena. After the final coding schemes were developed, tests of intercoder reliability were conducted among members of the research team. All transcripts and other qualitative records used in the tests were randomly selected and were removed from the pool once drawn.

"Memoing"[4] was also part of our analytic approach. This was a process we began at the outset of data collection through recording certain observations and ideas in our theory notebook. Later, as data analysis progressed, these theory notes were rewritten in the form of extensive memos that connected our thoughts on different phenomena and were later used as part of theory building, for which emphasis was placed on identifying negative cases or anomalies that refuted the theoretical framework established for the investigation. Diagramming was a key element of the analytic process that consisted of typologizing, matrix making, concept charting, and flowcharting (Lofland & Lofland 1995). These strategies enabled us to "visually represent relationships between concepts" (Strauss & Corbin 1990) and were part of theory building.

To prepare data for analysis, pseudonyms and codes were established for all participants and any other agencies or persons named in the ethnographic records. Taped interviews were transcribed verbatim according to standard procedures. Two software packages were used during data analysis: "Nudist" was used to create the coding scheme and code the qualitative data; "SPSS" was used for analyzing quantitative data and for qualitative data that were amenable to statistical analyses. In addition to the sense-making propositions, we examined our qualitative data for such themes as best practices and indicators of social capital, and analyzed our quantitative data for such patterns as the relationship between users' perceptions of how they were helped by the digital CI and their willingness to access it again for help in similar situations.

Trustworthiness: Reliability and Validity

To ensure the reliability and validity of our research we rigorously implemented measures recommended by Lincoln and Guba (1985) and Sandstrom and Sandstrom (1995) as appropriate to either the naturalistic or the positivist paradigm. Reliability is "the consistency or stability of a measure or test from one use to the next" (Vogt 1993). In this research we judged the reliability of our data by taking several measures. Specifically, reliability was increased through: (1) consistent note taking; (2) exposure to multiple and different situations when studying participants; and (3) comparing themes as they emerged from the data with findings from previous studies on related phenomena. For naturalistic inquiries, Lincoln and Guba (1984) proposed the concept "dependability" be used in place of reliability, and that the "audit trail" be used to ensure it. Similar to Chatman's (1992) use of note taking, the audit trail entails the researchers keeping scrupulous field notes and constantly comparing them with the other types of collected data for internal consistency. As a further means of ensuring reliability (or dependability), we audio-recorded the interviews and focus groups, used intracoder and intercoder checks in the analysis, and analyzed the data for incidents of observer effect.

Validity "pertains to truth or the degree to which the researcher is given a true picture of the phenomenon being studied" and it is important because it indicates the "extent to which findings may be generalized [and] it assist[s] the researcher in the analysis and interpretation of data" (Chatman 1992). The ways in which validity is discussed and verified differ among paradigms. For example, in naturalistic inquiry Lincoln and Guba, under the more general concept of "trustworthiness," use the concepts "credibility" and "transferability" to refer roughly to the concepts "internal validity" and "external validity," respectively. Chatman (1992), on the other hand, in the language of quantitative researchers, uses the subcategories of face, criterion, and construct validity in her ethnographic research. In light of the many recommendations found in the literature for ensuring validity, we implemented the following procedures in our research:

1. To ensure face validity, we asked whether the observations made "sense because they fit into an expected or plausible frame of reference" when we analyzed the data (Chatman 1992).
2. To ensure criterion and internal validity (or credibility) we pretested our instruments; had prolonged engagement in the field; engaged in rigorous note taking; used triangulation of methods (observation, interviews, and note taking); used peer debriefing; used negative case analysis; and used member checks or participant verification (Lincoln & Guba 1985, Sandstrom & Sandstrom 1995).
3. To ensure external validity, we aimed at providing "thick description" and a comprehensive description of the methods and theory used in the research so other researchers can determine whether the findings can be compared with those of their own studies.
4. To ensure construct validity, that is, "the analysis stage of field work in which a phenomenon has meaning in light of the conceptual framework guiding the study" (Chatman 1992), we examined the data with respect to Dervin's sense-making theory and principles of information behavior seeking found in the library and information science literature.

Summary

To obtain the most accurate and comprehensive view possible of how public libraries are delivering CI at the turn of the century, we used several methods that relied heavily upon the participation of many different individuals and organizations throughout the country. Their enthusiastic support for our work was, in our view, in large part due to librarians' eagerness to tell "their story" about their CI work along with users' and service providers' interest in expressing how they have benefited from these efforts.

REFERENCES

1. In-depth interviewing, which is a method used predominantly in qualitative research, consists of "repeated face-to-face encounters between the researcher and informants directed toward understanding informants' perspectives on their lives, experiences, or situations as expressed in their own words . . . [in which] the interviewer, not an interview schedule or protocol, is the research tool" (Taylor & Bogdan 1984).

2. Observing participants in their natural setting is a standard method used in qualitative research (Atkinson & Hammersley 1994) that "allows the researcher to discover the here-and-now interworkings of the environment via the use of the five human senses" (Erlandson et al. 1993).

3. According to Taylor and Bogdan (1984) an interview guide is "not a structured schedule or protocol, [but] a list of general areas to cover with each informant. The researcher decides how to phrase questions and when to ask them. The guide serves solely to remind the interviewer to ask about certain things and can be expanded or revised" as additional interviews are conducted.

4. Miles and Huberman (1994) cite the following definition of memoing by Glaser as classic: "The theorizing write-up of ideas about codes and their relationships as they strike the analyst while coding . . . it can be a sentence, a paragraph or a few pages . . . it exhausts the analyst's momentary ideation based on data with perhaps a little conceptual elaboration."

BIBLIOGRAPHY

Agada, John. 1999. Inner-city gatekeepers: An exploratory survey of their information use environment. *Journal of the American Society for Information Science,* 50, 74-85.

Archee, Ray. 1995. Freenets: Community access for all? *Online Access,* 10(4), 43-49.

Atkinson, P., and M. Hammersley. 1994. Ethnography and participant observation. In N. K. Denzin and Y. S. Lincoln (Eds.), *Handbook of qualitative research* (pp. 248-261). Thousand Oaks, CA: Sage Publications.

Avis, Andrew W. 1995. *Public spaces on the information highway: The role of community networks.* Unpublished master's thesis, University of Calgary.

Baker, L. M., and K. E. Pettigrew (1999). Theories for practitioners: Two frameworks for studying consumer health information-seeking behavior. *Bulletin of the Medical Library Association,* 87(4), 444-450.

Baker, Sharon L., and Ellen D. Ruey. 1988. Information and referral services—attitudes and barriers: A survey of North Carolina public libraries. *Reference Quarterly,* 28(3), 243-252.

Bates, M. (1989). The design of browsing and berrypicking techniques for the online search interface. *Online Review,* 13(5), 407-424.

Batt, Chris. 1996. The libraries of the future: Public libraries and the Internet. *IFLA Journal,* 22(1), 27-30.

Beamish, Ann. 1995. *Communities online: A study of community-based computer networks.* Unpublished master's thesis, Massachusetts Institute of Technology.

Benton Foundation and Libraries for the Future. 1997. *Local places, global connections: Libraries in the digital age.* Washington, D.C.: Communications Development.

Berkowitz, Rebecca, and Heather Brodie. 1996. Job searching on the Internet: A public library perspective. *Reference Librarian, 55,* 99-105.

Bertot, John C., and Charles R. McClure. 1996. *Sailor Network assessment final report: Findings and future Sailor Network development.* Maryland State Department of Education, Division of Library Development and Services. Available: http://research.umbc.edu/~bertot/sailor.final.report.pdf. Accessed December 5, 1998.

———. 1997. *Policy issues and strategies affecting public libraries in the national networked environment: Moving beyond connectivity.* Washington, D.C.: U.S. National Commission on Libraries and Information Science. Available: http://www.nclis.gov/what/publibpo. pdf. Accessed December 5, 1998.

———. 1998a. *The 1998 national survey of U.S. public library outlet Internet connectivity: Final Report.* Washington, D.C.: American Library Association and the U.S. National Commission on Libraries and Information Science. Available: http://istweb.syr.edu/~mcclure/survey98.pdf. Accessed January 6, 1999.

———. 1998b. *Victorian public libraries and the Internet: Results and issues.* Victoria, Australia: State Library of Victoria, VICLINK. Available: http://avoca.vicnet.net.au/~viclink/report97.htm. Accessed January 6, 1999.

Bertot, John C., Charles R. McClure, and Joe Ryan. 2001. *Statistics and performance measures for public library networked service.* Chicago: American Library Association.

Bishop, Ann P. 1997. Community networking questions. Available: http://www. lis.uiuc.edu/course/spring1997/450CI. Accessed February 20, 1998.

———. 1999. Making digital libraries go: Comparing use across genres. *International Conference on Digital Libraries: Proceedings of the fourth ACM conference on digital libraries,* August 11-14, 1999 (pp. 94-103), Berkeley, CA.

Bishop, Ann P., et al. 1999. Public libraries and networked information services in low-income communities. *Library and Information Science Research* 21, 361-390.

————. Socially Grounded User Studies in Digital Library Development. First Monday. Available: http://www.firstmonday. org/issues/issue5_6/bishop/index.html. Accessed May 2000.

Bishop, Ann P., Nancy A. Van House, and B. Buttenfield. (In Press). *Digital library use: Social practice in design and evaluation.* Cambridge, MA: MIT Press.

Bluming, Avrum, and Phillip S. Mittelman. 1996. Los Angeles Free-Net: An experiment in interactive telecommunication between lay members of the Los Angeles community and health care experts. *Bulletin of the Medical Library Association, 84,* 217-222.

Borgstrom, Amy. 1998. Community networks in the U.S.: At the cross-roads? Paper presented at the European Alliance for Community Networking Conference, July 1998, Barcelona.

Chatman, Elfreda. 1985. Information, mass media use and the working poor. *Library and Information Science Research, 7,* 97-113.

————. 1990. Alienation theory: Application of a conceptual framework to a study of information among janitors. *RQ, 29,* 355-368.

————. 1992. *The information world of retired women.* Westport, CT: Greenwood Press.

————. 1996. The impoverished life-world of outsiders. *Journal of the American Society for Information Science, 47,* 193-206.

————. 1999. A theory of life in the round. *Journal of the American Society for Information Science, 50,* 207-217.

————. (submitted). Theory building in library and information science.

Chen, Ching-Chih., and Peter Hernon. 1982. *Information seeking: Assessing and anticipating user needs.* New York: Neal-Schuman.

Childers, Thomas. 1975. *The information-poor in America.* Metuchen, NJ: Scarecrow Press.

————. 1984. *Information and referral: Public libraries.* Norwood, NJ: Ablex.

Chow, Clifton, et al. 1998. *Impact of CTCNet affiliates: Findings from a national survey of users of community technology centers.* Newton, MA: Community Technology Centers' Network. Available: http:// www.ctcnet.org/impact98.htm. Accessed December 18, 1998.

Cisler, Steve. 1994. Community networks: Past and present thoughts. In Steve Cisler (Ed.), *[Proceedings of the first] ties that bind: Building community networks* (pp. 29-37), Apple Conference Center. Cupertino, CA: Apple Library.

———. 1996. Weatherproofing a great, good place. *American Libraries,* 27(9), 42-46.

Clark, Dawn E. 1997. A comparison of health information on Florida's free-nets. *Bulletin of the Medical Library Association,* 85, 239-244.

Cohill, Andrew, and Andrea L. Kavanaugh (Eds.). 1997. *Community networks: Lessons from Blacksburg, Virginia.* Norwood, MA: Artech House.

Council on Library Resources. 1996. *Public libraries, communities and technology: Twelve case studies.* Washington, D.C.: Council on Library Resources.

Darton, Robert. The new age of the book. *New York Review of Books,* March 18, 1999. Available: http://www.nybooks.com/nyrev/WWW archdisplay.cgi?19990318005F. Accessed November 9, 2000.

Dervin, Brenda. 1992. From the mind's eye of the user: The sense-making qualitative-quantitative methodology. In Jack D. Glazier and Ronald R. Powell (Eds.), *Qualitative research in information management* (pp. 61-84). Englewood, CO: Libraries Unlimited.

Dervin, Brenda, and Michael Nilan. 1986. Information needs and uses. *Annual Review of Information Science and Technology,* 21, 3-33.

Dervin, Brenda, et al. 1976. *The development of strategies for dealing with the information needs of urban residents: Phase I: The citizen study.* Final report of Project L0035J to the U.S. Office of Education. Seattle, WA: University of Washington, School of Communications. ERIC: ED 125640.

Durrance, Joan C. 1984a. *Armed for action: Library response to citizen information needs.* New York: Neal-Schuman.

———. 1984b. Community information services: An innovation at the beginning of its second decade. *Advances in Librarianship,* 13, 99-128.

———. 1985. Spanning the local government information gap. *RQ,* 25, 101-109.

———. 1994. *Meeting community needs through job and career centers.* New York: Neal-Schuman.

————. 1997. Reinventing the community information professional: Strategies and approaches used to develop community networking knowledge. 1997 Annual Conference of the Association for Library and Information Science Education (February 12-14, 1997, Washington, D.C.).

Durrance, Joan C., and Karen E. Pettigrew. 2000. Community information: The technological touch. *Library Journal,* 125(2), 44-46.

Durrance, Joan C., and Karen G. Schneider. 1996. *Public library community information activities: Precursors of community networking partnerships.* Ann Arbor, MI: School of Information, University of Michigan. Available: http://www.si.umich.edu/Community/taos paper.html. Accessed March 5, 1997.

Durrance, Joan C., et al. 1993. *Serving job seekers and career changers: A planning manual for public libraries.* Chicago: American Library Association.

Elliott, Susan. 1995. Alaskans go sledding on the Internet. *PNLA Quarterly,* 59(2/3), 23-24.

Erdelez, S., and K. Rioux. 2000. Sharing information encountered for others on the Web. *New Review of Information Behaviour Research: Studies of Information Seeking in Context,* 1, 219-233.

Erlandson, David A., et al. 1993. *Doing naturalistic inquiry: A guide to methods.* Thousand Oaks, CA: Sage Publications.

Fichter, Darlene, and Colleen Martin-Brownell. 1997a. Community networks and health information providers: A natural partnership. *Health Care on the Internet,* 1, 5-21.

————. 1997b. Partners in health: The Saskatoon Free-Net and local health information providers. *Bibliotheca Medica Canadiana,* 18, 132-136.

Fietzer, William. 1996. Only connect: Community networks, libraries, and the case of Charlotte's Web. *Against the Grain,* 8(5), 1, 14, 16, 18.

Flynn, Suzanne. 2000. *Annual Report.* Multnomah County Auditor's Office. Available: http://www.co.multnomah.or.us/aud/Annual%20 Report%202000/Web%20Annual%20Report%202000.pdf. Accessed February 18, 2001.

Fox, Carol J. 1995. The public library on the electronic frontier: Starting a community online information system. *Illinois Libraries,* 77, 195-209.

Gall, Carole F., and Ellen G. Miller. 1997. Strategic planning with multi-type libraries in the community: A model with extra funding as the main goal. *Bulletin of the Medical Library Association, 85,* 252-259.

Gallimore, Alec. 1997. The Manchester Community Information Network. *The Electronic Library, 15,* 297-298.

Gates Foundation. 1999. Gates library initiative. Available: http://www.glf.org/about/default.html. Accessed January 6, 1999.

Geffert, Bryn. 1993. Community networks in libraries: A case study of the Freenet P.A.T.H. *Public Libraries, 32,* 91-99.

Glaser, B. G., and A. L. Strauss. 1967. *The discovery of grounded theory: Strategies for qualitative research.* Chicago: Aldine.

Gonzalez, Madelaine. 1998. Definition of community networking. *Community Networking, 1*(1), 1.

Granovetter, Mark S. 1973. The strength of weak ties. *American Journal of Sociology, 78,* 1360-1380.

———. 1982. The strength of weak ties: A network theory revisited. In Peter V. Marsden and Nan Lin (Eds.), *Social structure and network analysis* (pp. 105-130). Thousand Oaks, CA: Sage Publications.

Gray, Suzanne M. 2000. Virtual reference services: Directions and agendas. *Reference and User Services Quarterly, 39,* 365-376.

Gross, M. (In Press). Imposed information seeking in school library media centers and public libraries: A common behavior? *New Review of Information Behaviour Research: Studies of Information Seeking in Context.*

Grover, Robert, and Jack Glazier. 1986. A conceptual framework for theory building in library and information science. *Library and Information Science Research, 8,* 227-242.

Guard, Roger, et al. 1996. An electronic consumer health library: NetWellness. *Bulletin of the Medical Library Association, 84,* 468-477.

———. 1997. A community approach to serving health information needs: NetWellness. *Health Care on the Internet, 1,* 73-80.

Guy, Neil K. 1996. *Community networks: Building real communities in a virtual space?* Unpublished master's thesis, Simon Fraser University.

Hale, Charles. 1996. "Project MILLIKInet" becomes "DecaturNet": A library initiated community information network. *Illinois Libraries,* 78, 201-206.

Hallam, Emma, and I. R. Murray. 1998. World wide web community networks and the voluntary sector. *The Electronic Library,* 16, 183-190.

Hampton, K., and B. Wellman. 2000. Examining community in the digital neighbourhood: Early results from Canada's wired suburb. In T. Ishida and K. Isbister (Eds.), *Digital cities: Technologies, experiences, and future perspectives* (pp. 475-492). Berlin: Springer-Verlag.

Harris, Roma M. 1988. The information needs of battered women. *RQ,* 28, 62-70.

Harris, Roma M., and Patricia Dewdney. 1994. *Barriers to information: How formal help systems fail battered women.* Westport, CT: Greenwood Press.

Harsh, Stephen. 1995. *An analysis of Boulder Community Network usage.* Available: http://bcn.boulder.co.us/community/resources/harsh/harshproject.html. Accessed January 17, 1997.

Harvey, Kathy, and Tom Horne. 1995. Surfing in Seattle: What cyber-patrons want. *American Libraries,* 26, 1,028-1,030.

Head, A. J. (1999). Design wise: A guide for evaluating the interface design of information resources. Medford, NJ: CyberAge Books.

Hernon, Peter, and Ellen Altman. 1998. *Assessing service quality: Satisfying the expectations of library customers.* Chicago: American Library Association.

Howley, Kevin. 1998. Equity, access, and participation in community networks: The case for human computer interaction. *Social Science Computer Review,* 16, 402-410.

Hubbard, Bette A., et al. 1996. Newest members of the Net Set: Pittsburgh's Carnegie cashes in on community information. *American Libraries,* 121(2), 44-46.

Institute of Museum and Library Services. 2000. *Perspectives on outcome based evaluation for libraries and museums.* Washington, D.C.: The Institute.

Janes, Joseph, et al. 1999. Digital reference services in academic libraries. *Reference and User Services Quarterly,* 40(1), 145-150.

Janes, Joseph W. (In Press). Digital reference services in public and academic libraries. In Charles McClure and John Carlo Bertot (Eds.), *Evaluating Networked Information Services: Techniques, Policy, and Issues.* American Society for Information Science.

Jokitalo, Päivi. 1997. Building a virtual public library in Finland: Internet connections in Finnish public libraries. *Scandinavian Public Library Quarterly,* 30(3), 25-28.

Julien, Heidi. 1996. A content analysis of the recent information needs and uses literature. *Library and Information Science Research,* 18, 53-65.

Kindel, C. 1995. *Report on evaluation of definitions used in the public library statistics program.* Washington, DC: National Center for Education Statistics, U.S. Department of Education.

Knox, Sheryl C., and Joan C. Durrance. 1997. Pulling together: Technology, community and the public library. Ann Arbor, MI: School of Information, University of Michigan. Available: http://www.flint.lib.mi.us/gfcni/report. Accessed January 13, 1998.

Kochen, Manfred, and Joseph C. Donohue (Eds.). 1976. *Information for the community.* Chicago, IL: American Library Association.

Kunstler, James Howard. 1993. *Geography of nowhere: The rise and decline of America's man-made landscape.* New York: Simon and Schuster.

Kuokkanen, Martti, and Jukka Savolainen. 1994. The growth of sociological theories: A structuralist alternative to seeking theoretical continuity. *Quality and Quantity,* 28, 345-370.

Lilly, Erica B., and Connie Van Fleet. 2000. Measuring the accessibility of public library home pages. *Reference and User Services Quarterly,* 40(2), 156-165.

Lincoln, Y. S., and E. G. Guba. 1985. *Naturalistic inquiry.* Thousand Oaks, CA: Sage Publications.

Lofland, J., and L. H. Lofland. 1995. *Analyzing social settings: A guide to qualitative observation and analysis.* Belmont, CA: Wadsworth.

Maas, Norman L., and Dick Manikowski. 1997. *Guidelines for establishing community information and referral services in public libraries* (4th ed.). Chicago: American Library Association; Public Library Association.

Maciuszko, Kathleen L. 1990. A quiet revolution: Community online systems. *Online,* 14(6), 24-31.

Maine's Guide to Performance Measurement. 1999. Augusta, ME: Bureau of the Budget and State Planning Office.

Mansfield, Meribah. 1997. Ohio's OPLIN: The future of library service? *Library Journal,* 122(16), 44-47.

Marcella, Rita, and Graeme Baxter. 1999. The citizenship information needs of the UK public: The quest for representativeness in methodological approach. In T. D. Wilson and D. K. Allen (Eds.), *Exploring the contexts of information behaviour: Proceedings of the Second International Conference on Research in Information Needs, Seeking and Use in Different Contexts.* Sheffield, UK: 1998.

Mattison, David. 1994. Librarians and the Free-Net movement. *Computers in Libraries,* 14, 46-50, 52.

Miles, M. B., and A. M. Huberman. 1994. *Qualitative data analysis: A sourcebook of new methods.* New York: Sage Publications.

McClure, Charles, Joe Ryan, and William E. Moen. 1993. The role of public libraries and the use of Internet/NREN information services. *Library and Information Science Research,* 15, 7-34.

McClure, Charles R., and John C. Bertot. 1997. *Evaluation of the Online at PA Libraries Project: Public access to the Internet through public libraries.* Harrisburg, PA: Pennsylvania Department of Education, Office of Commonwealth Libraries. Available: http://research. umbc.edu/~bertot/OnLinePA.html. Accessed December 8, 1998.

―――. 1998. *Public library use in Pennsylvania: Identifying uses, benefits, and impacts.* Harrisburg, PA: Pennsylvania Department of Education, Office of Commonwealth Libraries. Available: http://istweb. syr.edu/~mcclure/pasectionlinks.html. Accessed December 8, 1998.

McConnaughey, James W., and Wendy Lader. 1998. *Falling through the Net II: New data on the digital divide.* Washington, D.C.: National Telecommunications and Information Administration. Available: http://www.ntia.doc.gov/ntiahome/net2/falling.html. Accessed December 15, 1998.

McKechnie, Lynne, and Karen E. Pettigrew. 1998. Theories for the new millennium: The deployment of theory in LIS research. In Elaine G. Toms (Ed.), *Information science at the dawn of the millennium:*

Proceedings of the 26th annual conference of the Canadian Association for Information Science (June 3-5, 1998, Ottawa, ON) (pp. 125-142). Toronto: CAIS.

McLeod, Marilyn. 1997. COIN—Columbia Online Information Network. *Against the Grain,* 9(2), 71-72.

Mehra, B., et al. 2000. The role of use scenarios in developing a community health information system. *Bulletin of the American Society for Information Science,* 26(4).

Milio, Nancy. 1996. Electronic networks, community intermediaries, and the public's health. *Bulletin of the Medical Library Association,* 84, 223-228.

Morgan, Janice C. 1997. *Community ties and a community network: Cupertino's computer-mediated Citynet.* Unpublished master's thesis, San Jose State University.

Morino, Mario. 1994. Opening doors of opportunity in the communications age. Available: http://www.morino.org/under_sp_ope.asp. Accessed February 16, 2001.

Morson, Ian, Joy Harrison, and David Cook. 1996. Boldly venturing into cyber space. *Library Association Record,* 98, 150-151.

National Telecommunications and Information Administration. 1999. The Telecommunications and Information Infrastructure Assistance Program (TIIAP): Program overview. Available: http://www.ntia. doc.gov/otiahome/tiiap/index.html. Accessed January 18, 1999.

Newby, Gregory A., and Ann Peterson Bishop. 1996. Community system users and uses. In Steve Hardin (Ed.), *Proceedings of the 59th Annual Meeting of the American Society for Information Science* (Oct. 21-24, 1996, Baltimore, MD) (pp. 118-126). Medford, NJ: Information Today.

Newton, Robert, Ala MacLennan, and J. D. Allison Clark. 1998. Public libraries on the Internet. *Public Library Journal,* 13(1), 2-7.

Ontario Ministry of Culture and Communications. 1991. *Review of access to human services information.* Toronto, ON: Queen's Printer for Ontario.

Ormes, Sarah, and Charles R. McClure. 1997. A comparison of public library Internet connectivity in the USA and UK. In Sarah Ormes and L. Dempsey (Eds.), *The Internet, networking, and the public library* (pp. 24-40). London, England: Library Association.

Osborne, David, and Ted Gaebler. 1992. *Reinventing government: How the entrepreneurial spirit is transforming the public sector from schoolhouse to statehouse, city hall to the Pentagon.* Reading, MA: Addison Wesley.

Palmour, Vernon, et al. 1979. *Information needs of Californians.* Rockville, MD: King Research.

Patrick, Andrew. 1996. Services on the information highway: Subjective measures of use and importance from the National Capital FreeNet. Available: http://debra.dgbt.doc.ca/services-research/survey/services. Accessed February 12, 1997.

————. 1997. Media lessons from the National Capital FreeNet. *Communications of the ACM,* 40(7), 74-80.

Patrick, Andrew S., and Alex Black. 1996a. Implications of access methods and frequency of use for the National Capital Freenet. Available: http://debra.dgbt.doc.ca/services-research/survey/connections. Accessed February 20, 1997.

————. 1996b. Losing sleep and watching less TV but socializing more: Personal and social impacts of using the NCF. Available: http://debra.dgbt.doc.ca/services-research. Accessed February 20, 1997.

Patrick, Andrew S., Alex Black, and Thomas E. Whalen. 1995. Rich, young, male, dissatisfied computer geeks? Demographics and satisfaction with the NCF. In D. Godfrey and M. Levy (Eds.), *Proceedings of Telecommunities 95: The international community networking conference* (pp. 83-107). Victoria, BC: Telecommunities Canada. Available: http://debra.dgbt.doc.ca/services-research/survey/demographics/vic.html. Accessed February 20, 1997.

Patton, Michael Quinn. 1997. *Utilization-Focused Evaluation.* Thousand Oaks, CA: Sage Publications.

Pettigrew, Karen E. 1996. Nurses' perceptions of their needs for community information: Results of an exploratory study in southwestern Ontario. *Journal of Education for Library and Information Science,* 37, 351-360.

————. 1997a. I and R in the electronic age: Bringing it to the classroom. 1997 Annual conference of the Association for Library and Information Science Education (February 12-14, 1997, Washington, D.C.).

————. 1997b. *The role of community health nurses in providing information and referral to the elderly: A study based on social network theory.* Unpublished Ph.D. dissertation. Faculty of Graduate Studies, The University of Western Ontario.

————. 1997c. Frameworks for studying information behavior: A unit theory specification of Granovetter's strength of weak ties. In Bernd Frohmann (Ed.), *Communication and information in context: Proceedings of the 25th Annual Conference of the Canadian Association for Information Science* (June 8-10, 1997, St. John's, NF) (pp. 131-154). Toronto, ON: CAIS.

————. 1999. Waiting for chiropody: Contextual results from an ethnographic study of the information behavior among attendees at community clinics. *Information Processing and Management, 35,* 801-817.

Pettigrew, Karen E., and Margaret Ann Wilkinson. 1994. Controlling the quality of community information: An analysis of the effects on dissemination of the differences between I and R agencies and community networks. *Information and Referral, 16,* 185-194.

————. 1996. Control of community information: An analysis of roles. *Library Quarterly, 66,* 373-407.

Pratt, Jennifer S. 1997. Public libraries: An important piece in the community network puzzle. *North Carolina Libraries, 55*(1), 12-14.

Putnam, Robert D. 1995. Bowling alone: America's declining social capital. *Journal of Democracy, 6,* 65-78.

————. 2000. *Bowling alone: The collapse and revival of American community.* New York: Simon and Schuster.

Raskin, J. (2000). *The humane interface: New directions for designing interactive systems.* Reading, MA: Addison Wesley.

Rathbone, Daniel B. 1997. Disseminating transportation information. *Transportation Quarterly, 51,* 117-128.

Resnick, Robert. 1997. Community information resources in United States public libraries: A study and survey. *Public Libraries, 36,* 218-229.

Robbins, Jane, and Douglas Zweizig. 1988. *Are we there yet? Evaluating library collections, reference services, programs, and personnel.* Madison, WI: School of Library and Information Studies, University of Wisconsin-Madison.

Roberts, Robert A. 1996. *The diffusion of innovation: Dualities of one electronic free community network.* Unpublished master's thesis, University of Oregon.

Roger, Eleanor J., and George D'Elia. 2000. The impacts of the Internet on public library use: An analysis of the current consumer market for library and Internet services. Available: http://www.urban libraries.org/pdfs/finalulc.pdf.

Roger, Nancy K. 1998. Redefining reference services: Transitioning at one public library. *Reference and User Services Quarterly,* 38(1), 73-75.

Ross, Catherine Sheldrick, and Kirsti Nilson. 2000. Has the Internet changed anything in reference? The library visit study, phase 2. *Reference and User Services Quarterly,* 40(2), 147-155.

Ryan, Elizabeth A. 1996. *Creating a rural community network: A case study.* Unpublished master's thesis, University of New Brunswick.

Sales, G. 1994. *A taxonomy of human services: A conceptual framework with standardized terminology and definitions for the field* (3rd ed.). Los Angeles, CA: Information and Referral Federation of Los Angeles County and the Alliance of Information and Referral Systems.

Sandstrom, A. R., and P. E. Sandstrom. 1995. The use and misuse of anthropological methods in library and information science research. *Library Quarterly,* 65, 161-199.

Savolainen, Reijo. 1993. The sense-making theory: Reviewing the interests of a user-centered approach to information seeking and use. *Information Processing and Management,* 29, 13-28.

———. 1995. Everyday life information seeking: Approaching information seeking in the context of "way of life." *Library and Information Science Research,* 17, 259-294.

———. 1998. Use studies of electronic networks: A review of the literature of empirical research approaches and challenges for their development. *Journal of Documentation,* 54, 332-351.

———. 1999. Seeking and using information from the Internet. The context of non-work use. In T. D. Wilson and D. K. Allen (Eds.),

Exploring the contexts of information behaviour: Proceedings of the Second International Conference on Research in Information Needs, Seeking and Use in Different Contexts (Sheffield, UK, August 13-15, 1998) (pp. 356-370).

Schalken, Kees, and Pieter Tops. 1994. The digital city: A study into the backgrounds and opinions of its residents. Paper presented at the Canadian Community Networks Conference, August 15-17, 1994. Carleton University, Ottawa, ON. Available: http://cwis.kub.nl/~frw/people/schalken/schalken.htm. Accessed December 3, 1998.

Schuler, Douglas. 1994. Community networks: Building a new participatory medium. *Communications of the ACM, 37*, 39-51.

———. 1996. *New community networks: Wired for change.* New York: Addison-Wesley.

Schumer, Douglas. 1997. Let's partner as patriots. *American Libraries, 28*(8), 60-62.

Schwabe, Gerhard. 1997. Citizenship information in Norway, Germany, and from the European Commission: The need and its delivery. In Pertti Vakkari, Reijo Savolainen, and Brenda Dervin (Eds.), *Information seeking in context: Proceedings of an international conference on research in information needs, seeking and use in different contexts* (August 14-16, 1996, Tampere, Finland) (pp. 434-448). London, England: Graham Taylor.

Stapleton, Kathy. 1997. Local government information and the Internet. *Australasian Public Libraries and Information Services, 10*(1), 21-41.

Stearns, Susan. 1996. The Internet-enabled virtual public library. *Computers in Libraries, 16*(8), 54-57.

Strauss, A. L. 1987. *Qualitative analysis for social scientists.* New York: Cambridge University Press.

Strauss, A. L., and J. Corbin. 1990. *Basics of qualitative research: Grounded theory procedures and techniques.* Thousand Oaks, CA: Sage Publications.

Straw, Joseph E. 2000. A virtual understanding: The reference interview and question negotiation in a digital age. *Reference and User Services Quarterly, 39*, 376-380.

Surak, Kristin. 1998. *A cross-cultural comparison of community computer networks.* Unpublished honors thesis, Florida State University.

Taylor, S., and R. Bogdan. 1984. *Introduction to qualitative research*. New York: John Wiley.

Thompsen, Philip A. 1997. *Toward a public lane on the information superhighway: A media performance analysis of the community-wide education and information service initiative*. Unpublished master's thesis, University of Utah.

Toms, Elaine G., and Mark T. Kinnucan. 1996. The effectiveness of the electronic city metaphor for organizing the menus of Free-Nets. *Journal of the American Society for Information Science*, 47, 919-931.

Tuominen, Kimmo, and Reijo Savolainen. 1997. A social constructionist approach to the study of information use as discursive action. In Pertti Vakkari, Reijo Savolainen, and Brenda Dervin (Eds.), *Information seeking in context: Proceedings of an international conference on research in information needs, seeking and use in different contexts* (pp. 81-96). London, England: Graham Taylor.

Vakkari, Pertti. 1997. Information seeking in context: A challenging metatheory. In Pertti Vakkari, Reijo Savolainen, and Brenda Dervin (Eds.), *Information seeking in context: Proceedings of an international conference on research in information needs, seeking and use in different contexts* (pp. 451-464). London, England: Graham Taylor.

————. 1998. Growth of theories on information seeking: An analysis of growth of a theoretical research program on the relation between task complexity and information seeking. *Information Processing and Management*, 34, 361-382.

Vakkari, Pertti, and Martti Kuokkanen. 1997. Theoretical growth in information science: Applications of the theory of science to a theory of information seeking. *Journal of Documentation*, 53, 497-519.

Van House, Nancy, et al. 1987. *Output measures for public libraries: A manual of standards and procedures*. Chicago: American Library Association.

Vaughan, Misha W., and Nancy Schwartz. 1999. Jumpstarting the information design for a community network. *Journal of the American Society for Information Science*, 50(7), 588-597.

Vogt, P. 1993. *Dictionary of statistics and methodology.* Thousand Oaks, CA: Sage Publications.

W. K. Kellogg Foundation. 1998. *W. K. Kellogg Foundation evaluation handbook.* Battle Creek, MI: W. K. Kellogg Foundation. Available: http://www.wkkf.org/Publications/evalhdbk/default.htm.

———. 1999. A Kellogg Foundation cross-cutting theme: Information systems/technology. Available: http://www.wkkf.org/Programming Interests/InfoSys/default.htm. Accessed January 18, 1998.

Wagner, David G., and Joseph Berger. 1985. Do sociological theories grow? *American Journal of Sociology,* 90, 697-728.

Warner, Edward S., et al. 1973. *Information needs of urban residents.* Baltimore, MD: Regional Planning Council.

Weil, Stephen, and Peggy Rudd. 2000. *Perspectives on outcome based evaluation for libraries and museums.* Washington, D.C.: Institute of Museum and Library Services.

Welling, Penny H. 1996. Introducing the Internet in a rural setting. *North Carolina Libraries,* 54, 165-168.

Wellman, B. 2001. Physical place and CyberPlace: The rise of networked individualism. *Journal of Urban and Regional Research,* 25(2), 227-252.

Wellman, B., et al. 2001. Does the Internet increase, decrease, or supplement social capital? Social networks, participation, and community commitment. *American Behavioral Scientist,* 45.

Wening, Tony. 1997. The Missouri Express: A link to the online information world. *Missouri Library World,* 2(1), 2-4.

Westat. Feb 1999. *Evaluation Report for U.S. Department of Commerce: National Telecommunications and Information Administration.* Telecommunications and Information Infrastructure Assistance Program: 1994 and 1995 Grant Years. Washington, D.C.

———. March 2000. *Evaluation Report for U.S. Department of Commerce: National Telecommunications and Information Administration.* Technology Opportunities Program: 1996 Projects. Washington, D.C.

Wilson, Myoung C. 2000. Evolution or entropy? Changing reference/ user culture and the future of reference librarians. *Reference and User Services Quarterly,* 39, 387-391.

Wilson, Tom. 1997. Information behavior: An interdisciplinary perspective. *Information Processing and Management,* 33, 551-572.

Witte, J. C., L. M. Amoroso, and H. Pen. 2000. Research methodology—Method and representation in Internet-based survey tools—Mobility, community, and cultural identity in Survey 2000. *Social Science Computer Review,* 18(2), 179-195.

Woods, Deb. 1996. The I and R heart of community-wide networks: HelpNet, a model under construction. *Information and Referral,* 18, 7-19.

Wyman, Steven, John C. Beachboard, and Charles R. McClure. 1997. *User and system-based quality criteria for evaluating information resources and services available from federal websites: Final report.* Dublin, OH: OCLC Online Computer Library Center, Office of Research.

Yerkey, A. Neil. 1997. Librarians and community computer networks: A training institute. *Journal of Education for Library and Information Science,* 38, 116-127.

Zhang, Y. 2000. Using the Internet for survey research: A case study. *Journal of the American Society for Information Science,* 51(1), 57-68.

Zweizig, Douglas. 1979. The informing function of adult services in public libraries. *RQ,* 18, 240-244.

Zweizig, Douglas, and Brenda Dervin. 1977. Public library use, users, uses: Advances in knowledge of the characteristics and needs of the adult clientele of American public libraries. *Advances in Librarianship,* 7, 231-255.

Zweizig, Douglas, et al. 1994. *Tell It! Evaluation sourcebook and training manual.* Madison, WI: School of Library and Information Studies, University of Wisconsin-Madison.

Index

Joan C. Durrance is professor at the University of Michigan School of Information. Her research and teaching interests include information needs and use, public libraries, community information systems, professional practice, and the evaluation of information services. Her various research projects include two grants—"Help Seeking in an Electronic World" and "How Libraries and Librarians Help"—developed jointly with Karen Pettigrew and funded by the federal agency, Institute of Museum and Library Services (IMLS).

Durrance is a past-president of the Association for Library and Information Science Education. Her research has earned her ALA's Isadore Gilbert Mudge–R.R. Bowker Award given for a distinguished contribution to reference librarianship.

Karen E. Pettigrew is an assistant professor at the Information School of the University of Washington. Her main research and training area is in information behavior and the social and cognitive aspects of how people need, seek, give, and use information in different contexts. She recently studied how community health nurses link the elderly with local services, and how people use the Internet for daily problem solving. She also studies the use of theory in LIS research and teaches qualitative research methods and community analysis. Pettigrew received PhD (1997) from the University of Western Ontario and held a postdoctoral fellowship, funded by the Social Sciences and Humanities Research Council of Canada, at the University of Michigan's School of Information (1998–99).

WITHDRAWN

WITHDRAWN

WITHDRAWN

Z 716.4 .D87 2002x

Durrance, Joan C.

Online community information